MW01518396

The Best of

Estate Law Canada

Lynne Butler, BA LLB TEP

Copyright @2015 by Lynne Butler

All rights reserved.

No part of this book may be reproduced or transmitted in any form by any means graphic, electronic, or mechanical without permission in writing from the publisher, except by a reviewer who may quote brief passages in a review. Any requests for photocopying, recording, taping or information and retrieval systems of any part of this book shall be directed in writing to the publisher. Contact www.butlerwillsandestates.com for more information.

Printed in the U.S.A.

First edition 2015

ISBN 978-1-329-65075-6

Table of Contents

Introduction

I first started blogging in 2009, and I had no idea what I was doing. I loved the idea of connecting with people and talking to them about wills and estates law, so I just dived in. I learned on the job, so to speak. Nobody read it at first. I remember avidly poring over the daily statistics and being thrilled to pieces when ten people read my blog in one day.

Early posts on the blog were Alberta-centric. This is because I lived and worked in Alberta and at the time I couldn't imagine that anyone outside that province would be interested in reading my words. Once I realized that people were reading from all across Canada, I stopped focusing just on one province and started addressing the entire country. Since then I've had readers from as far away as England, USA, Australia, Hungary, Turkey, France, Germany, the Netherlands, India, Ukraine, Russia and the Philippines.

I never thought I'd one day have posts that had each been read by more than 200,000 people. At the time this book was compiled, about 4,000 readers a day were accessing my blog, and I had just passed the 3.3 million view mark. The blog has grown steadily, and I hope will continue to grow for some time yet to come.

Many times, I've heard or seen bloggers comment about how hard it is to keep thinking of things to blog about. I've never had that problem. There never seems to be a shortage of topics, though there is often a shortage of time to cover them all. I'm naturally a chatty person, which I'm sure surprises nobody. My daughter has remarked that I can get conversation out of a turnip. I love to talk about wills and estates topics in particular, so a blog is a natural thing for me.

I blog about what I work with every day: wills, estates, powers of attorney, elder law, trusts, probate, estate disputes, loss of capacity, planning. I suppose with a net that wide, it would be difficult to run out of things to say. My blog posts are inspired by cases I'm working on at the office, questions people ask me at seminars, or things I've seen in the news. Sometimes I get on a bit of a rant, and end up using my backspace key to erase my original words and replace them with more moderate ones. At one point, I started answering reader's questions in the form of new blog posts, because that gave me so much more room to answer them. Readers seem to enjoy those.

Occasionally I post things that really don't have anything to do with wills and estates. They are usually cartoons or little videos that I find funny and I think will give someone a smile. Once I posted a video of a young man who went dancing in the street and was hit by a car (he was okay). I posted it, and immediately second-guessed myself, wondering whether I'd upset anyone. But readers seemed to like it, based on the viewership stats. Wills and estates are serious topics and a little joke now and then just lightens us all up.

At times, I've written blog posts at 3 a.m. because I was sleepless with worry over some case at work (and I usually proofread them the next day because fatigue negatively affects my ability to spell and to string sentences together). I've written many posts from hotel rooms in the evenings before giving early seminars at towns and cities other than my home. I've even posted a few from my cell phone while waiting to board airplanes. I've never had a proper blog schedule, as such. Sometimes a week goes by while I'm just too busy to put hands on the keyboard, and at other times I've posted two or even three topics in one day. I've often seen social media experts talking about the need to commit to a regular blogging schedule, but that has just never worked out for me.

I've always felt that the key to blogging successfully was to be myself. I blog the way I talk, and I write the way I talk. I'm straightforward, and usually kind to people, and I like to get right to the heart of things. I've been told many times over the years that I "don't sound like a lawyer" and I'm convinced that the people who say that mean it as a compliment. They only mean that they can easily understand me. I want to speak and write in a way that people understand. I want to *communicate*, not just put words on a page. Fortunately, that seems to come easily to me.

Blogging has been a give-and-take experience for me. I knew from day one that I didn't necessarily want to blog for other lawyers who, I assumed, know as much as I do about the topics. I wanted to write for executors trying to figure out their next step, beneficiaries who needed to know what the heck was going on, and adult kids whose parents were starting to have memory issues. These are the people who had always been my clients in real life, and the people who came to my seminars. I've always tried to stay focused by asking myself what readers want to know.

The questions posed on my blog sometimes challenged me to learn more about certain topics, and that's never a bad thing. While I want to educate my readers, in a way they've been educating me.

From reading their feedback and their questions, I've learned that no matter where people are, and no matter how big or small the estate, the issues are the same. The emotions are the same. We're all just people, and estate disasters affect us all the same way. Keeping up this blog has made me a better seminar speaker, and a better lawyer, as it has deepened my understanding of the individuals caught up in estate issues.

The workings of the blog itself are a mystery to some readers. The feature that seems to trip up many of them is that their comments don't show up until I've clicked on them. The blog itself tells readers that fact, and most of them get it. However, there are some who don't see the notice and end up posting their comment three or four times. After that, they either give up in disgust, or email me to tell me that they couldn't make the blog work. I post their comment, and just delete the duplicates. I figure they're too intent on the issue or question that's bothering them to worry about the mechanics of a site.

I use that feature to ensure that I can keep spammers out. I don't get an enormous amount of spam, but even a few spam posts are too many. The ones I seem to get the most frequently are the testimonials about the power of love gurus who can make straying husbands come back. Why they think an estate planning blog is a suitable hunting ground for that kind of message, I don't really know.

Not all reader comments get published. Every now and then I get a rambling, sometimes profane rant about someone's sister or uncle who is the rottenest, most crooked executor ever born. I choose not to publish them for a couple of reasons. The first is potential poster's remorse. I figure at least some of those people wrote in a fury, posted in haste, and have since calmed down. They probably don't really want their words out there, especially if the facts make the case and the parties identifiable. Venting is fine, but not everyone needs to see it. Hopefully the act of venting just to me relieved some of the pressure.

From a purely selfish point of view, I don't want to be dragged into the middle of somebody's libel suit.

Eventually I realized that a number of junior lawyers and articling students were reading my blog. Many would email me or come up to me at Canadian Bar Association events and tell me that they had found this or that post useful in a case they were working on. I really appreciated those comments. Some ask me to discuss specific issues with them, which I always do. I assume they're getting ready to impress the boss, or perhaps the client, and I don't mind helping someone with that. I also hear sometimes from senior lawyers who drop into my blog now and again. I'm glad of that, since I read their blogs, too.

Occasionally I'm asked why I blog. I think the answer to that question has changed over time. I started because the publicist at my book publisher urged me to, and because I wanted the dialogue I thought it would bring. Over time, I've found blogging immensely rewarding in so many ways. I thrive on the interaction. I'm getting to know some of the regular commenters. I really feel connected to what consumers of legal services want to know about. I think that some people are helped by my words, and that feels wonderful. I sometimes get feedback from readers with words like "thank you" and "bless you" and "thank God for you" and I know I've done something good for someone. It's my little way of doing something positive in the world.

I decided to compile this book partly because passing three million readers felt like a milestone. It also seems timely as I enter a new phase of my career in a new place, with a new business of my own. It's almost like holding a birthday party for myself.

I hope that having a collection of the most-read posts will make it easier for readers to find what they want to read. Obviously these are the posts that readers find to be the most useful. I thought that by distilling the last six years' worth of blog posts down to the ones that people read the most (and share the most) would be a great time-saver for readers, and a convenient way of keeping the most important information close at hand.

With each post that is reproduced in this book, I mentioned the number of views the post had garnered as of the day I put this book together. The number is changing constantly, as readers browse through older posts on specific topics. My blog has about 2,200 posts. This book features 80 of them.

Also in this book, you'll find updates of some posts, and commentaries on some others.

Putting this book together also helps me and my readers move forward. I found it fascinating to realize that more than 204,000 people read a post called "Does Canada have death or inheritance taxes?" That's an awful lot of people who aren't getting the information they need from direct sources such as an estate lawyer, an accountant, or even from Canada Revenue Agency's webpage. In fact, everything I post about taxation is heavily read, even though I cannot answer some questions that really need the expertise of an accountant.

Another astonishingly popular post is called "Joint tenants vs tenants in common", which has more than 200,000 views. For a while I was surprised that so many people had questions about title to property but I came to realize just how little people understand about their assets in general.

It's just one of those things that nobody pays any attention to until something forces them to focus on it.

Seeing the steady readership of certain posts helps me understand what readers want and need from me. On the flip side, posts about topics that I thought would appeal, such as business succession planning, were sadly under-read compared to others. All of this information helps me put out blog posts that help readers with their own issues. I know I can't give legal advice to all of these folks, but at least I can steer some of them in the right direction.

I hope to be talking about wills and estates for many more years. I dedicate this book to all of those readers who have taken this journey with me so far, and to those who will join me in the future.

Executor "how-to"

By far the most popular type of post on my blog is what I call "executor how-to". I talk about how to get information, how to prepare an inventory, how to communicate with the beneficiaries, how to get a Tax Clearance Certificate, and hundreds of other things that executors need to know. Anything that helps an executor figure out what to do, or what not to do, is read by thousands of people. I find that stories about executors who were punished by the courts, and links to resources for executors are also gobbled up.

I know that many readers are acting in an executor capacity, because they tell me so in their questions and comments. But sometimes I wonder why these executors are not getting better advice or at least more information from the lawyers hired to help them with the estates. I've concluded that it's at least in part the lawyers' fault, because the hourly rate charged is just too much for most executors to pay. Either the executors don't ask questions, or they accept answers without really understanding them because they are trying to keep costs down.

It has always been the case that people have supplemented the information provided by their lawyers with their own research, and that's what some executors do with this blog.

I also think that a lot of beneficiaries read the executor how-to posts. Recently someone asked me what I blog about the most. I replied that the most common topic is how executors can do what they need to do. The second most common topic is how to stop executors from doing what they are doing. In many cases, beneficiaries are reading about what executors are supposed to do because they're involved in an estate and don't understand what the executor is doing.

Estates are really hard on most beneficiaries. Harder than most executors realize. At least an executor has the estate lawyer to talk to, whereas the beneficiaries don't have any guidance at all. They rely on the executor for information, and believe me, it's not always forthcoming. Nor is it always accurate or complete.

All in all, it makes sense that "executor how-to" would be a popular type of post, since it applies to so many of us in one way or another.

What are the executor's duties?

99,236 views

When I talk about executor's duties in this blog, I usually focus on one duty or one detail at a time. However, I think many executors out there would appreciate having an overview of their duties, either as a first-time checklist, or as a refresher of what they learned when they first began working on the estate. So here is a list of what an executor in Canada is supposed to do (note that an administrator appointed by the court has to do these things as well, though he or she cannot do them until they are appointed):

- make arrangements for the disposition of the deceased's remains, as well as any arrangements for funeral, memorial service, etc.

- find out the names and addresses of the beneficiaries and notify them of their interests in the estate.

- list the contents of any safety deposit box owned by the deceased

- make an inventory of all of the assets and debts of the deceased. Give all assets and liabilities a value as of the date of death.

- check that property is insured. Advise the insurance company of the death. Place additional insurance if necessary.

- secure any valuable estate property. Once smaller valuable items have been inventoried, put them somewhere safe where they can't be stolen or damaged.

- arrange for protection and supervision of vacant land and buildings.

- make arrangements for the proper management of estate assets. If there is a business or farm, make sure there is someone running it properly. Sell assets if appropriate.

- apply for a Grant of Probate or Grant of Administration.

- hire a lawyer to advise you on any complicated or unclear issues.

- apply for all pensions, death benefits, life insurance or any other benefits that are payable to the deceased's estate.

- if there is any jointly owned property, advise the other joint tenant of the deceased's death (notice that this list does not include you taking care of the transfer of title. The surviving joint tenant can do that).

- if there are any life insurance policies, RRSPs or any other assets that name a beneficiary other than the estate, notify that beneficiary of the deceased's death.

- pay all of the debts and expenses owed by the deceased and by the estate.

- decide whether or not to advertise for creditors and claimants. If you choose to advertise, do so in accordance with the law. If there are claims, check them out for legitimacy. Pay legitimate claims from the estate.

- determine how much tax the deceased owes. Have tax returns prepared and filed on time. Pay the taxes before paying beneficiaries. Get a Canada Revenue Agency tax clearance certificate.

- if there is a lawsuit against the estate, hire a lawyer and run the lawsuit on behalf of the estate.

- set up any trusts directed by the Will. Administer the trusts for the length of time and on the conditions set out in the Will.

- answer enquiries from residuary beneficiaries, creditors and other stakeholders.

- prepare executor's financial statements including a proposed compensation schedule and a proposed final distribution schedule.

- distribute the deceased's property in accordance with the Will or with intestacy law.

As you can see, many items on this list are going to break down into smaller lists with several items of their own, but this should give you a general idea of what you'll be expected to do as an executor.

Does an executor have to pay the deceased's unpaid debts out of his own money?

7,271 views

This isn't going to be a quick yes or no answer because, as with everything in law, much depends on the circumstances of each case. Here are some general rules you can work with.

The debts of an estate (including income tax) must be paid before any beneficiaries receive their money. If an executor ignores the debts and pays the beneficiaries, the executor may be held personally liable for those debts.

If paying the debts first means that the beneficiaries get little or nothing out of the estate, this is not the executor's fault.

Often an executor asks me about debts because there are more debts than there are assets in an estate. An executor should a) honestly try to figure out what legally enforceable debts exist, b) be very careful to put appropriate values on estate assets, and c) use the estate assets to pay the debts. Where there is a lot of debt, this usually means selling assets to realize a cash value that can be divided among creditors. If there is not enough money to pay everyone 100% of what is owed to them, the executor may have to try to negotiate a settlement whereby each creditor gets a certain amount on the dollar.

If the estate is fully used up to pay the legally enforceable debts and expenses, and there are still debts of the deceased unpaid, the executor does not have to use his own money to pay them. That's assuming, of course, that the executor has not done anything fraudulent or negligent with the estate's money.

13

When listing the debts of an estate, the executor should remember to include debts that are not payable immediately but that will become payable in the future, such as income tax at the end of the year.

To protect himself or herself against personal liability, an executor should advertise in the newspaper for creditors and claimants against the estate. Doing so won't overcome any negligence on behalf of the executor, but assuming there is no negligence, advertising for creditors certainly helps.

What happens with a bankrupt estate?
5,839 views

First of all, it's important to realize that there is a difference between an insolvent estate and a bankrupt estate. An insolvent estate, which is much more likely, simply does not have enough assets to pay all of the debts. A bankrupt estate has actually declared bankruptcy.

When talking about either insolvent or bankrupt estates, I often hear people comment that nobody needs to do anything about it because obviously there are no assets. But that's not necessarily true. A deceased person could have a half-million dollar home and another half-million in investments, but if he or she has more than a million dollars in debts and liabilities, there isn't going to be enough money to pay all the creditors. So even though there are assets, the estate is still insolvent. And someone still has to sell that house and cash in those investments on behalf of the deceased person and pay out the proceeds.

That person is the executor named in the Will. If there is no Will, there should be an administrator appointed by the court in the usual way.

Usually in an insolvent estate, the executor will negotiate with the creditors to come to an agreement as to how much each will get. Often everyone agrees to a certain amount "on the dollar" so that they'll each recover at least part of the debt. It's to everyone's advantage not to turn it into a lawsuit, because fighting it out in court means the resources of the estate, which are already not enough, will end up being spent on legal fees and court fees.

If after an executor starts working on the insolvent estate, it is petitioned into bankruptcy by the creditors or the

15

executor declares that the estate is bankrupt, the executor will have to step out of the picture. The control of the assets and debts will be handed over to the Trustee in Bankruptcy to deal with. The executor's claim for compensation can be added to the other claims against the estate.

UPDATE: WHEN A BENEFICIARY IS BANKRUPT, HIS WHOLE SHARE IS PAID TO THE BANKRUPTCY TRUSTEE, WHO WILL THEN GIVE BACK ANY PART OF THE INHERITANCE NOT NEEDED TO PAY THE DEBTS.

What is an executor's year?

7,739 views

The "executor's year" is a rule of thumb. It refers to the fact that most estates should be wrapped up within a year of the executor getting a Grant of Probate, or an administrator getting a Grant of Administration.

One reason this rule of thumb exists is to remind executors that they don't have forever to take care of the estate. Beneficiaries and creditors have a vested interest in having matters concluded, and the executor is responsible for taking care of that.

Another reason we have the rule is to remind beneficiaries that estates cannot be wound up overnight. There is much more for an executor to do than most people realize, and some of it is truly time-consuming. Also, some of the matters that fall within the executor's responsibility rely on others to conclude, such as selling a house. You can't sell a house without a buyer, and the executor is only going to have so much control over that.

More complicated estates take longer. In some estates there are long-term leases to wind up, businesses to be sold, assets in other countries to deal with, or disputes about who is going to get what. You can expect those estates to take longer than others.

The effect of the rule is that a beneficiary who doesn't want to wait for his or her inheritance cannot force the executor to pay out his or her share within the executor's year. Nor is interest required to be paid by the estate on that inheritance until after the year is up.

The rule is meant to be workable for your average executor who is doing the best he or she can with the estate. However, we all know there are a few executors out there who refuse to do anything, leaving the estate and the beneficiaries at a standstill. Once the year is up, an unpaid beneficiary can take legal steps to have the estate administered. This could mean removing the executor entirely, requiring that a full accounting be prepared, or a dozen other things depending on the situation.

I am asked about the executor's year by beneficiaries and not usually by executors. If you are a residuary beneficiary who is frustrated with an executor who is not taking action, you might want to talk to an estate lawyer about it.

What does an executor do about creditors and claimants?

5,870 views

Executors on many estates publish a notice called Notice to Creditors and Claimants in the newspaper in the area where the deceased lived. The purpose is to find out if there are any debts "out there" that the executor doesn't know about. As debts of an estate must be paid before beneficiaries may be paid, paying out the estate before knowing about all debts could end up in a mess.

The Notice to Creditors and Claimants directs anyone who believes that the deceased owed him or her money to contact the executor within a time specified in the notice. I've noticed that most articles and information on this topic stop there. They don't tell an executor what to do if someone makes a claim. This article is intended to take the information a little further.

If the executor believes that the claim is a legitimate claim, the executor may accept it and pay it from estate funds. This might mean waiting until there are funds available in the estate, but most creditors would rather wait to get the money than not get it at all. If the Inventory of the estate has not yet been filed with the court, the executor should add the valid claim to the inventory as a debt, and then pay it along with all other estate debts.

The executor may not be sure that a claim is valid, particularly if he or she has not had a lot of involvement with the deceased's financial affairs prior to the deceased's death. The executor may then require the claimant to verify the claim by producing a receipt, work order, written agreement, I.O.U or whatever paperwork is available. If the executor still thinks that the claim is invalid or that the amount of the claim is wrong, he or she can serve a notice on the claimant that requires the claimant to come up with some conclusive proof. If that proof is not given within a certain time (in Alberta it's 60 days), the claim is lost. This means the claim can never be made again, as it is legally barred.

In practice, most claimants will send the supporting paperwork along with the claim in the first place, as it is just common sense to do so. It's rare that an executor ends up serving a notice to contest the claim.

What's the executor's role with respect to assets that pass outside the estate?

3,381 views

Not everything owned by a person will form part of his or her estate upon death. For example, if the deceased was an owner of jointly owned property and the other joint owner is still alive, then the joint property is not part of the deceased's estate. The surviving joint owner will have complete ownership. This rule applies to joint real estate and joint financial assets, such as bank accounts.

Another example is an asset with a beneficiary that was designated by the deceased while he or she was alive. For most estates, this means an RRSP, RRIF, LIRA, life insurance policy and/or a pension. When the deceased passed away, the person named in the asset became entitled to ownership of the funds. (Note that this does not apply to an RESP, which behaves differently).

When assets owned by the deceased are going to be owned automatically by someone else and are not controlled by the deceased's Will, they are said to "pass outside of the estate". An executor is appointed by a Will to take care of the assets in the estate. So what is an executor supposed to do about the assets that pass outside of the estate?

The executor will not be able to deal with those assets as it will be beyond his or her legal role to sign the necessary documents or to receive the funds. The executor's role is more or less to provide notification, information and documentation to others so that they can deal with the assets.

The executor must let each of the holders of the assets - the holders being the banks, insurance companies, etc. - know that the deceased has passed away. This should be done in writing by providing a copy of the Death Certificate. The funds will not be sent to the executor for handling and in most cases the executor won't even be kept in the informational loop about what is happening with the assets. But if the executor has in a timely manner provided the necessary information that allows others to get on with business that will cause the deceased's plans to be carried out, then the executor has fulfilled his or her duty.

In the matter of joint property, the executor can simply notify the other joint owner(s) of the deceased's death, provide a copy of the Death Certificate, and ask that the surviving joint owner deal with the asset. After that, it's up to the surviving joint owner to get the asset switched into their name alone.

How to list the contents of the deceased's safety deposit box

2,296 views

Many advisors - myself included - have repeatedly told executors that once the deceased has passed away, the executor must check the safety deposit box. But do you know what you're checking for? What are you supposed to take out of there and what are you supposed to leave? Are you supposed to give away the things you find in the box? This post will give you some general information about how to treat the deceased's safety deposit box.

Shortly after the deceased's death, the executor should call the bank and make an appointment to see the box. Note that spouses and next-of-kin are not entitled to do this if they are not joint owners of the box and are not named executors. In the majority of cases, the family members have a pretty good idea who the executor is.

If the original will hasn't yet been found, it's a good idea to check the box very soon so that if the will is in the box, the right executor can be identified.

This is a bit of a quandary at times. Nobody can go into the deceased's safety deposit box except for the executor, but you don't know who the executor is until you open the box and read the will. If this is the case, make an appointment at the bank and take a copy of the death certificate with you. You may find that the bank staff will keep the contents of the box confidential from you while they look into the box to see whether you are in fact the executor.

Once you have established that you are the executor and there is a safety deposit box, your first duty is to list the contents of the box. This is done at the bank in the presence of a bank staff member who acts as a witness. Listing the contents is exactly what it sounds like - making a detailed list of everything in the box.

This must be a detailed list. There is no point to making a listing that just includes "papers and personal items".

Describe the papers. Some common examples:
- title deed to the deceased's home or cottage (include address or legal description)

- Canada Savings Bonds (include bond serial numbers, face value)

- insurance policies (include name of insured, name of company, policy number, face value)

- stock certificates (include name of stock, number of shares)

Many people also keep small valuables such as jewelry, precious metals and small family heirlooms in their safety deposit boxes. Describe the items as fully as you can. Some of these items might have been given away specifically in the deceased's will (such as when a mother leaves a precious ring to her daughter). If that's the case, you may leave the items there until you have progressed with the estate to the point where you are ready to distribute the personal items.

Consider the ownership of the box. Is there another owner of the box? If so, you will have to work with that owner to determine which of them owns which items. This is not too hard to figure out with paperwork, but it's more challenging with items like jewelry.

In your first visit, you will probably not take out anything except for the original will (and as mentioned, only the executor named in the will can legally do this). That is enough to get started on the executor's duties. Make sure that before you leave the bank, you have changed the ownership of the box to the deceased's estate so that you can access it again in the future

One of the executor's duties is to keep valuables safe, so many executors leave the items and papers in the safety deposit box until they are needed. Consider who else has access to the box when determining whether this is the safest place to keep the items. If anything goes missing, you are personally responsible for it.

If your list is detailed enough, you will be able to get started on the probate documents without having to go back and look at the paperwork again. Eventually, of course, all items will be removed as you wind up the estate, but for most estates that is a few months down the road.

Where do I find the deceased's accounts and investments?

3,142 views

A reader has asked me a question that I hear frequently, so I'm sharing the question and my answer with all of you. Here's the question:

> *"When a person passes away, how do you locate all their accounts and investments if you don't have an updated list? Is it as simple as using their SIN card to locate them?"*

I don't think you're going to like my answer, because there is nothing simple or easy about this. It usually takes a lot of legwork to find a deceased's assets and liabilities.

Having the SIN card is definitely helpful, as banks and other asset-holders can search their databases using a SIN card. This can be helpful since many people may have the same or similar name, but only one person will have a particular social insurance number. It should make searching easier.

The problem is determining which banks or brokers or investment advisors to ask. There is no place that you can enter a SIN and come up with a comprehensive list of everything a person owns in various institutions. You will have to ask one bank or advisor at a time. It used to be worse; at least these days you can go to any branch of a bank and get a search of all branches of that bank. In the not-so-distant past you had to approach each branch individually.

So how do you know which banks or advisors to ask?

Check paperwork at the deceased's home and office. Look for statements and bank books of course, but also any correspondence such as insurance offers.

In these days of paperless banking, fewer and fewer people leave paper statements around. If you don't have access to the deceased's computer, you're going to have to do it the hard way.

If you see a credit card in the deceased's wallet, check the bank that issued the card. People frequently get credit cards from the same place they do their regular banking.

Check to see which banks have branches close to the deceased's home or place of work. Most people choose to bank where it's convenient for them. Seniors in particular tend to choose the branch closest to home, within walking distance if possible.

If you have access to the deceased's past tax records, check to see which banks issued T5 slips for investments. There should be a copy of each T5 attached to the deceased's copy of a filed return.

When you check with a bank, whether or not you are successful in locating a bank account, ask the personnel to check the bank's investment arm as well. The major banks all have investment advisors attached to them (Scotia McLeod, RBC Dominion Securities, etc.). Also remember to ask about safe deposit boxes, because many people will store original share certificates, deeds to the house etc. and you can often find clues there. For example, look at the deed to the house to see whether there is a mortgage registered against the house; the title will tell you which bank holds the mortgage.

Remember that many people have assets in more than one bank. So the fact that you've located an account in, say, Scotiabank, doesn't mean that you should stop looking.

The cold hard fact is that it is often an immense amount of work to figure out what another person owned, particularly where most records are kept on a computer that you can't access. This is why estate planners are always suggesting that people make an updated list of assets and liabilities.

As I said, you're probably not enjoying this answer one little bit, but unfortunately there may not be an easier way.

UPDATE: USING A WRITTEN RECORD SUCH AS "FOR MY FAMILY, WITH LOVE" CAN SAVE YOUR EXECUTOR AND FAMILY MEMBERS MANY HOURS OF SEARCHING.

Can I sell estate property before getting probate?

10,657 views

Because it can take weeks to receive a Grant of Probate from the courts, and because executors are usually under pressure from beneficiaries to wrap up the estate quickly, executors are often in a hurry to sell the house or other property in the estate. This is particularly true if the market is in the seller's favour at the time. They don't always want to wait until they've received the paperwork from the court.

Unfortunately, the executor does have to wait for the actual court order. It's not just a technicality or insignificant piece of paper. Think about what it actually does. It allows someone else to sell a person's house and look after the money. If a Probate order wasn't needed, then what would stop pretty much anyone from trying to sell that house and keep the money? The probate order is proof that the person selling the house, who after all is not the owner of it, has the legal right to sell it and accept the money.

An executor who goes ahead without the probate and tries to sell a property will find that the Land Titles Office or registry will not allow this to happen. They must have a court certified copy of the probate before they will register a new owner.

This doesn't mean that the house can't be listed for sale while the probate documents are being processed at the court. The executor who is selling the house just needs to make sure that he or she is clear on the sales agreement that the sale is subject to a probate order being granted.

Beneficiaries who are pressuring for the sale of the house need to realize that once the executor has filed the documents and is waiting for the probate order to be issued, there is little the executor can do to speed up the process.

How and when to set up an estate bank account
19,679 views

Most executors and administrators of estates will at some point set up a bank account for processing financial transactions on the estate. Even when an executor or administrator has hired a lawyer to apply to the court for probate or administration, he usually still has to set up an account. The alternative is to run all transactions through the lawyer's trust account, which becomes expensive.

When the account is opened will depend largely on whether you are an executor (i.e. appointed by a valid will) or an administrator (i.e. appointed by the courts in the absence of a valid will). An administrator has no authority whatsoever to take charge of the deceased's money until he or she is appointed by the court. In other words, he or she can't open an account until the court provides them with a document putting them in charge.

If you're an executor, however, you can open the account at any time once you take charge of the estate. Your authority to do this comes from the will, not the probate. The name on the account should make it clear that this is not your personal money and that you are holding it in the name of the estate. If the deceased is John Smith and you, the executor or administrator, are Mary Smith, the account should be called either "The Estate of John Smith" or "Mary Smith, Executor of the Estate of John Smith".

Executors usually don't wait for the court to issue a probate document before opening the account. While the probate application is being processed, you, as executor, will usually apply for the CPP death benefit, collect any outstanding wages, benefits and refunds, and pick up any cash lying around the deceased's home. All of those things and more may be deposited into the estate account before the grant of probate is issued. As time goes on, you will add other assets to the account, such as when you cash in GICs, sell the deceased's home or transfer over the proceeds of the deceased's bank account.

If you receive cheques made out to the deceased person, they don't have to be re-issued to the estate. They can be deposited to the estate account as they are.

Can the executor sell an estate property to a family member?

6,182 views

An executor who is looking after the estate of someone who has just passed away has the obligation to gather in all of the assets of the deceased, pay the bills and distribute the remaining property to the beneficiaries. Usually the executor must deal with the house or condo owned by the deceased. Most likely he will sell the house and divide the net proceeds among the beneficiaries. But what if one of those beneficiaries, a family member of the deceased, wants to buy the house rather than having it sold outside the family? Can the executor do that?

The executor must first look to the will to see whether there is anything in the will that would prevent this. For example, the house might be left to one of the beneficiaries as their inheritance, either outright or in a trust. Or the will might state that a certain beneficiary has a specific amount of time to come forward with an offer to purchase, during which time nobody else can buy it. This might happen if the deceased had felt that more than one of the children might be interested in the family home, or if there is something unique about the property, such as a farm or family cottage.

Another option, although a rare one, is that the deceased might have specifically directed that the estate be liquidated, possibly to prevent any of the beneficiaries from owning any particular property.

If the will doesn't specifically prevent the executor from selling to a family member, the executor can go ahead and arrange to sell the property to the family member. It must be sold at fair market value, in other words, the price it would fetch if it were sold on the open market. (Executors would be well advised to protect themselves by getting two or three appraisals before agreeing on a price).

The executor must always remember that the beneficiaries can't receive anything from the estate until the deceased's debts have been paid, so it's possible that the house is needed for paying debts. In that case, the family member who wants the house is out of luck.

If the family member who wants to buy the house is a beneficiary, and the house is worth less than the beneficiary's total inheritance, the beneficiary can simply choose to take the house instead of cash. For example, the beneficiary's share of the estate might be worth $500,000, while the house is worth $400,000. Instead of taking $500,000 cash, the beneficiary might want to take the house plus $100,000.

If the beneficiary's share is less than the value of the house, the beneficiary may still use his or her inheritance to buy the house. For example, if the beneficiary's share is going to be $200,000, and the house is worth $400,000, obviously the beneficiary can't simply take the house. But he or she would only have to pay $200,000 for the house, as the other $200,000 is coming out of the estate.

Don't try this without the help of an estate lawyer!

One last thing that might cause a problem for the executor is a lack of powers and authorities in the will. This is a section of the will in which your estate planning lawyer examines your goals as stated in the will, and the assets you own, and includes the legal wording that will make sure your wishes are carried out in the most effective way possible. This is almost always missing from home-made wills, and frankly, sometimes even in the wills drawn up by non-specialist lawyers.

For example, in many jurisdictions, the law says that if an executor needs to sell the house from an estate to pay the bills, he doesn't need anyone's permission. However, if the executor is going to sell the house for any other reason - such as to sell to the beneficiary discussed in this post - he does need permission. He needs the written ok of all residuary beneficiaries. If one of those beneficiaries is a minor, the permission needs to come from the Office of the Public Trustee.

Having said that, the lawyer drawing the will should have included a clause that dispensed with the otherwise needed permission.

If the account is frozen, how does the executor pay for the funeral?

8,885 views

Seminar season is in full swing for me, making me doubly busy but also letting me interact with even more people than I usually do. I always encourage questions from my audiences, and always get plenty of them. I notice than many listeners are interested in the mechanics of an estate - how things work, who does what, how long things take, etc.

At one recent seminar, there were questions about whether a deceased person's bank accounts are frozen at the time of death, and if so, whether an executor has to pay funeral and other expenses out of his own pocket.

If the deceased owned a joint bank account with right of survivorship, the account won't be frozen. The surviving joint owner will be able to continue to use the account as before. For tax, estate and other reasons, the surviving joint owner should make sure that the bank is alerted of the death of one owner and the name on the account adjusted to reflect the current situation.

If you are one of the thousands of Canadians who owns an account jointly with your parent or your child, be aware that there is no longer an automatic right of survivorship on these accounts. Though you may have been told by the bank when it was set up that there was a right of survivorship, the law has changed right across Canada. An inter-generational joint account where the parent put in the money and later added a child as a joint owner is considered to be held in trust for the parent's estate. That account will be frozen.

If you have an inter-generational joint account, talk to an estate planning lawyer or your bank manager to find out what you can and should do about it while both owners are still alive.

RRSP, RRIF and LIRA accounts are not generally frozen. They are normally paid to the named beneficiary. If they are payable to the estate, they may be frozen until the executor obtains a grant of probate.

The deceased may have had bank accounts or investment accounts in his or her own name. These account are normally frozen on the death of the owner. Once the executor obtains probate, the bank or investment advisor will release the funds to the executor.

As mentioned, the follow-up question to whether an account is frozen is whether an executor must pay estate expenses out of his own pocket. In particular, funeral bills were a concern, as they tend to amount to thousands of dollars. The good news is that if an executor or family member takes the funeral bill to the bank where the deceased held his account, the bank will pay the funeral bill directly from the deceased's money. The money won't be given to the executor or family member; it will be sent directly to the funeral home.

This holds true for other expenses as well, as long as they are obviously bills that the deceased would have had to pay, such as the utilities on the deceased's home. This is up to the individual bank branch to determine, but it's always worth asking.

"I'm contesting the will" - real threat or just bluster?

56,434 views

I hear a lot of talk from beneficiaries about contesting of wills. The idea is tossed out as a threat by individuals who are unhappily surprised by not getting what they had hoped for under a deceased's will. But is it a realistic threat? The impression I get is that many people believe that anyone who doesn't like a will can simply demand that the will be changed to suit them.

This is not how it works.

Contesting a will means applying to the appropriate court to have a will struck down as being invalid. You would have to prove your case with sufficient relevant evidence. No judge in the country is going to rubber-stamp your request just because that's what you want.

Though each case and each will is different, the general concepts behind contesting a will are the same everywhere. Each case falls within these general headings. They are:

- undue influence

- lack of mental capacity

- problems with the will document itself, such as improper witnessing, lack of signature, other formalities not observed.

You'll notice that I'm leaving aside the issues that lawyers usually refer to as "dependent relief". This refers to an application by a spouse or child to get a larger share of an estate under a valid will. The will itself would still stand, but the court is asked to give a larger portion of the estate to someone in the family.

In this post I'm talking about the ways in which someone hopes to bring the entire will crashing down.

Undue influence:
A person relying on the concept of undue influence aims to show that the will should be struck down because the deceased had been forced or persuaded to make a will that wasn't really what he or she wanted. The idea is that the person getting the estate under this will wouldn't receive it had the deceased been left alone to do what he or she really wanted to do, and therefore shouldn't be allowed to receive it now.

Lack of mental capacity:
Mental capacity is an essential component of a valid will. A person making a will must understand what he or she owns, must have an appreciation of his or her obligations and must understand the nature and effect of making a will. Therefore, a will can be attacked on the basis that the deceased didn't really know what he or she was doing due to illness, injury, medications or other causes of confusion.

One thing that should leap out at you when you read about undue influence or lack of mental capacity is just how hard it would be to prove that either of these factors actually existed when the will was made.

How do you prove that the son receiving the lion's share of his mother's estate manipulated her into leaving it all to him? He will say that he was the one who helped Mom the most during the latter part of her life and that she left the estate to him out of gratitude. Then the battle will begin in earnest.

You may be absolutely positive that he influenced her. You may even think that "everyone knows" he manipulated her. But we're talking about a court of law, not a family dinner table. How do you prove it?

I'm not saying that these cases never succeed, because they do. They rely on a judge's interpretation of doctor's reports, witness testimony, family history, common sense and the law. They are tough cases that take a long time, a lot of money and infinitely thick skin to tolerate, but when the evidence exists, they succeed.

But I also believe there is an awful lot of blustering and threatening going on, carried out by those who have no real idea of just how hard it really is to successfully contest a will. Most people who talk about contesting a will change their minds once they realize what's involved.

Executors collecting debts of the deceased
4,537 views

One of the many jobs that executors must do on the estate of someone who is deceased, is figure out what debts are owed to the deceased, and then collect them. I would rank this among the least enjoyable of executor's tasks (not that most of them are a barrel of monkeys, mind you).

Debts owed to the deceased can range from large (e.g. an insurance settlement from a car accident) to very small (e.g. a refund from the local newspaper once the subscription is cancelled).

The general rule is that the executor must collect all legally enforceable debts. Most debts owed to a person continue to be owed after that person passes away. This is why the executor, who represents the deceased, is the one who has to collect them.

There are a couple of ways in which the Will itself can help the executor:

One of the most common debts on an estate is a loan to one of the children that the deceased parent made during his or her lifetime. Ideally, the deceased parent has given the executor some direction in the Will about whether to collect the debt. If nothing has been said, then the executor is obligated to collect that loan. The executor doesn't have the legal authority to forgive that loan if the Will doesn't allow for that. This is a really difficult thing for the executor to deal with, especially if the executor and the beneficiary who owes the money are siblings.

A way of dealing with that debt, rather than actually collecting money from the beneficiary, is to reduce the amount of money the beneficiary is going to inherit.

If you are a parent who has lent money to a child, or a child whose parent has lent money, make sure the repayment (or not) of the loan is mentioned in the parent's Will. This may certainly help to cut down on disputes.

Another place where the Will itself can be very helpful to the executor is the section of the Will that contains powers or authorities for the executor. In some Wills, there is a power to settle this kind of matter as the executor sees fit.

This clause could be helpful where the amount of the debt owed to the deceased is so small that it will actually cost more time and money to collect it than it is worth. The existence of a small debt puts the executor between a rock and a hard place, because he or she is obligated to collect all debts owing, including the small ones. However, if the power referred to is included in the Will, this will allow the executor to decide that a given debt is just not worth it to collect.

All debts that are owed to the deceased, once collected, should be put into the executor's estate bank account that every executor opens up once he or she starts working on the estate. This keeps the estate's money separate from the executor's money and keeps the records straight.

Top Five Mistakes Made by Executors

147,022 views

Being an executor isn't easy. There's plenty of paperwork to be done, lots of interaction with government agencies, registries and lawyers. There are always beneficiaries putting on pressure to do things more quickly. And if all of that weren't tough enough, an executor risks personal liability for any mistakes he or she makes.

It's not surprising that executors make mistakes. In the interest of informing present and future executors, here is a look at the top five mistakes executors make:

1. Ignoring inconvenient or unpopular parts of the Will

Executors frequently feel that they have a better, or "more fair" idea of how an estate should be distributed than is directed by the Will. However, it's not their choice. Their job is to distribute the estate according to the Will, not to re-write it. An executor might be less tempted to change the distribution if he or she kept in mind that for every person who likes the new distribution, there is at least one person who is outraged by it. If the executor fails to follow the distribution under the Will, he or she may be responsible for paying the disappointed beneficiary out of his or her own personal funds.

Executors ignore other parts of the Will too. For example, an executor might sell an asset and give the beneficiary the proceeds, even though the Will directed that the asset be given in specie. The executor might give trust funds to children at a younger age than that directed in the Will. He or she might forgive loans that were to be collected. None of these things are within the authority of an executor and each exposes the executor to potential liability.

2. Keeping secrets and failing to communicate

Executors are often secretive to the point of being furtive. Nothing is going to fuel speculation and suspicion on the part of beneficiaries more than being kept in the dark. An executor must respond to reasonable enquiries from the residuary beneficiaries of an estate. They are entitled to it, and responsible for policing the actions of the executor. They are entitled to see the Will and all of the documentation filed with the court. Believe me, if beneficiaries can't get the information they're entitled to, they will suspect the worst. Perhaps executors don't realize that as soon as the frustrated beneficiary hangs up the phone, his or her next call is to a lawyer.

Time and time again I hear stories of family members who are presented with complicated, mysterious documents by an executor and being told to sign them, without being given any information about what's going on. Any executor who treats important legal issues this way should expect pushback from the beneficiaries. This is a textbook example of how to start an estate dispute.

The failure to communicate even reaches to co-executors. Sometimes a person will act for weeks or months as an executor and not reveal that there is a co-executor appointed until he or she is forced to do so because a financial institution refuses to go further without both signatures.

3. Treating estate money as their own

Perhaps this is the reason for the secrecy mentioned above, but many executors either don't know or ignore the limits of their role. Executors have been known to pay off their

44

own debts, make loans to family members and buy into business ventures, all with estate funds. None of this is lawful, and executors may be forced to repay those funds out of their own money.

Even executors who are honest make mistakes with estate money. For example, many executors don't see a problem with using estate funds to fly in family members from all over the world to attend the funeral, and using estate funds to supply those family members with hotels, transportation, meals and sometimes even clothing to wear to the funeral. These are not estate expenses. The executor could end up paying for all of that himself or herself.

4. Failing to deal with debts and taxes before paying beneficiaries

I suppose it's a natural human reaction to ignore unpleasant things, but this can't apply to executors who must prepare tax returns. By law, debts of an estate, including tax liability, must be paid before beneficiaries receive their shares. It isn't easy to resist the pressure from those who want their money now, but an executor who pays beneficiaries without having cleared all debts and liabilities may be personally responsible for paying those debts.

5. Trying to do everything cheaply

It's certainly not a bad idea to keep estate administration costs low, but unfortunately the way many executors go about that actually ends up costing the estate more money. "Keeping costs low" seems to translate into forgoing professional help in many cases. For example, they try to do tax returns without the help of an accountant, which means they miss eligible deductions and elections. They also miss filing deadlines, and so incur interest. They try to sell real estate without a realtor and settle legal disputes without a lawyer. They sell assets without appraisals and invest money with no guidance. Very few people can do all of these things well, particularly at the same time as keeping their full-time job and family going.

The best way to avoid these five main errors is to stick to the Will, take your time and ask for professional help when you need it.

Executor liability

12,472 views

Most people who act as an executor on an estate do so only once in a lifetime. This means that there are an awful lot of rookie executors out there doing their best to figure out what they are supposed to be doing. It's not easy.

An executor is personally liable for any losses he or she causes the estate. That means that if the executor is negligent or very slow-moving or reckless with any of the assets of the estate and that causes a loss in monetary value, the executor is personally on the hook for repaying the loss. The loss could be penalties and interest on a tax return that the executor filed extremely late for no good reason. It could be the purchase of a house where the executor sold the estate's house for much less than market value because he or she didn't bother getting estimates. It could be covering expenses such as meals or travel that should not be covered as they are not legitimate estate expenses.

This rule can be tough to translate into actual practice, because most people understand that an executor's expenses and legal fees are covered by the estate. This is often taken by inexperienced executors to mean they can charge every meal, every kilometer they drive, every item they purchase, to the estate, and that no matter what they do, they are backed by estate money. However, the estate will pay the reasonable costs and expenses of a proper administration. The estate will not pay for the executor's mistakes that could have been avoided with a little bit of attention. The estate won't pay for the executor's trip to Hawaii.

There is a line that can be crossed by an executor. There comes a point where the executor's behaviour is so unreasonable that it amounts to fraud or neglect. The courts deal with estates like this on a case-by-case basis.

If the executor has simply neglected to take care of things and monetary value has been lost, the executor could repay the loss by reducing or completely eliminating the pay he would otherwise have received for being the executor. If it goes beyond that, and the executor has behaved in an egregious way, foregoing the fee might not be enough. The executor could be held liable in court for losses that must be paid out of his own money.

If you are a beneficiary and you really believe that the executor on an estate you're involved in is causing losses to the estate, make an appointment to see an experienced estate planning lawyer. Take all the paperwork relating to the estate with you. Get an opinion on what, if anything, should be done about the executor.

If you are an executor and you are worried about your own liability, remember that if you are honest, let everyone know what you're doing, and move things along as quickly as is reasonably possible, you are not likely to run into trouble. You can also avoid losses and mistakes by relying on experienced professional help, such as accountants, lawyers, realtors and appraisers. That way you can back up your actions with documented proof of why you took the steps you took.

Most estates are wrapped up within a year (not including receipt of the final tax clearance certificate from Canada Revenue Agency), so this should be your goal. It might take longer if the estate involves selling a business, dealing with real estate in other countries, asking the court for clarification of things in the Will, etc.

UPDATE: EXECUTORS CAN ALSO CONTROL AND
LIMIT THEIR LIABILITY BY PURCHASING
EXECUTOR'S INSURANCE THAT COVERS LOSSES
TO THE ESTATE

Executor compensation - how do we know how much he/she can have?

36,180 views

It's fairly common knowledge that someone who acts as the executor of an estate can charge a fee for doing that job. What is less well known is how we can tell how much the person can charge.

When the deceased person has stated in the Will how much his or her executor is to receive for being the executor, the situation is clear. The amount stated in the Will is the appropriate amount. It can be expressed as a dollar amount or as a percentage of the estate. Unless something very unfortunate happens to the estate, such as being caught up in a lawsuit, the executor will be entitled only to the amount stated in the Will.

Executor's fees are over and above the reimbursement of out-of-pocket expenses incurred by the executor (I will post again on executor's expenses later, as there is often confusion about what expenses should be reimbursed).

If the executor is a trust company, the person making the Will will agree on a fee schedule with the trust company at the time the Will is made. The Will should state that an agreement was signed. That way, it is clear to all parties involved how much the person making the Will wanted the trust company to receive in fees.

Most Wills don't say how much an executor can charge. That being the case, the executor will have to claim his compensation near the end of his work as executor, as he is preparing to send the beneficiaries their shares of the estate. The executor will prepare financial statements showing all transactions in and out of the estate, along with a statement that sets out how he proposes to distribute the assets to finish the estate. Part of that proposal is his request for fees for himself. The residuary beneficiaries (that is, the beneficiaries who share in the residue of the estate) are asked to agree to the amount he has requested.

Most provinces and territories don't use a specific formula that tells executors how much they can charge. Most rely on statutes that use phrases such as "fair and reasonable compensation". This leaves the concepts of "fair" and "reasonable" open to interpretation. Quite often, the executor and the beneficiaries don't see eye to eye on the amounts.

UPDATE: ALTHOUGH THIS ARTICLE REFERS TO THE RANGE OF FEES IN ALBERTA, THAT RANGE APPLIES ALL ACROSS THE COUNTRY.

In Alberta, the accepted range of compensation is between 1% and 5% of the deceased's estate. Where an given executor falls within that range will depend on how complicated the estate is, whether there were any unique legal situations, the value of the assets, the amount of responsibility handled by the executor, how much time he or she put in, and other factors.

If the residuary beneficiaries think the claim is reasonable, they will agree in writing and the executor will take the proposed fee. If even one residuary beneficiary disputes the amount and it can't be negotiated to everyone's satisfaction, the amount may have to be set by a judge. If that happens, the estate pays for the lawyers to go to court and ask the judge to set the fee.

I encourage people making their Wills to think about including a clause stating how much your executor is to be paid. Talk to your lawyer about it if you want to discuss what is fair in your particular case. Remember that an experienced Wills lawyer will be able to give you ideas about how to handle pretty much any situation arising from an estate.

Executor's fees, lawyer's fees or both?

14,892 views

Today I'd like to answer another excellent question from a reader that I think will be of interest to many of you. The question is:

> *"Can a lawyer who writes up a will also be an executor of that will? Also, can he claim fees as both a lawyer and as the executor? And who decides how much the executor receives? If there are two executors, do they both get the same amount? Are there any limits to executor fees? Thanks."*

Yes, a lawyer who writes up a will can be the executor, though he should not witness the will if he is named as executor.

At the time the will is drawn, the lawyer will claim his usual fee for writing the will. Later, when the testator passes away and the lawyer acts as executor, he will claim an executor's fee, which would be the same as a non-lawyer would claim. The lawyer would only be able to claim a lawyer's fee on top of that if he did legal work for the estate that would have needed a lawyer in any event. For example, if a lawyer would have been hired to file for probate anyway, then the lawyer/executor (or his firm) can do that work and charge the usual lawyer's rate for that work.

When a lawyer or accountant is named as an executor, it's a good idea to include a clause in the will that specifically addresses the fact that they can be paid professional rates for professional work and not for their entire executorship. The lawyer and the accountant should already know what they can charge, but the other people involved in the will might not know.

If the will states how much an executor is to be paid, then that is how much the executor will receive. Occasionally the amount is set out in dollars, but usually it's expressed as a percentage of the estate. Unfortunately, plenty of wills don't address executor's fees.

If the will doesn't address executor's fees, the executor must fall back on the statute law and case law for guidance. Executor fees vary from province to province, though there are usually only general guidelines to follow. Estates vary widely, depending on the kind of assets, the value of assets, the number and location of beneficiaries, whether there are claims or difficulties, the expertise of the executor and a hundred other things. As a general rule, an executor is able to claim between 1% and 5% of an estate, with only the more complicated estates reaching the top of that range.

The amount the executor receives - within the range mentioned - is normally determined by the residuary beneficiaries of the estate. During the final accounting for the estate, when the executor is ready to cut the cheques to the beneficiaries, the executor should put forth in writing a proposal of the fees he or she wants to claim. The beneficiaries are asked to approve the estate accounting including the proposed executor's fee.

If the residuary beneficiaries think the fee is too high (and quite often that's the case) then the executor and the beneficiaries may be able to negotiate a sum that's satisfactory to everyone.

If they can't agree, the executor's fee must be set by the court. This involves a hearing in courtroom. The estate can't be distributed to the beneficiaries until that has happened because the fee may be set higher or lower than the executor had requested.

If there is more than one executor named, the fee is expected to be split among them. It's not always an equal split. Sometimes one executor has taken on more of the work because of geography, time or skill. The executors should work out between themselves how they are going to split the fee, and if they simply can't agree, it has to be decided by a judge.

When can the executor be reimbursed for expenses?

7,559 views

When an executor is compensated for his or her work on an estate, the amount he or she receives is separate from the reimbursement of expenses. Unless a will specifically says otherwise, the fee is over and above being paid back for expenses. In this post I'd like to look at the expenses rather than the fee.

It's always a good idea for an executor to try to limit his or her personal involvement with estate expenses by submitting bills directly to the bank where the deceased had an account. Many know that they can submit the funeral bill to the bank so that the bank pays that bill directly without the funds passing through the executor's hands. However, this arrangement also works for other bills that are clearly the deceased's bills, such as property tax for the deceased's home, or the final heat and electricity bills. It's worth a chat with a banking officer to see what can be done.

Of course, this idea only works when there is cash available in the deceased's account. Realistically there might not be enough funds. There are plenty of estates which consist of a house and a RRIF and not much more. In those cases, submitting bills isn't going to be helpful and the executor just might end up paying for things (funeral, lawyer, accountant, bills, or tax) out of his or her own money.

When hiring a lawyer to obtain a Grant of Probate, you will likely find that lawyers who do a lot of estate work won't even bill you until they get the Probate. This is because they know their bill should be paid by the estate and that you likely won't be able to liquidate estate assets unless you have the probate.

I always advise executors not to take their fee until the estate is finished and the fee has been approved either by the residuary beneficiaries or the court (except for very unusual circumstances). However, that's not the case with expenses which the executor pays directly out of pocket. When the executor is out of pocket, of course he or she needs to be reimbursed as quickly as possible. The executor doesn't have to wait for any specific time or event.

Being reimbursed from the estate means that money has become available, either because an asset has been sold or an investment has been collected in by the executor. These funds would have been deposited into the estate bank account set up by the executor around the time he or she applied for probate. This is where any reimbursement should be taken from. Keep the arrangements simple and transparent. Don't take money directly out of accounts or investments owned by the deceased.

I would suggest that the executor reimburse himself or herself once a month out of the estate account. This way ALL money taken by the executor can easily be accounted for in one statement, and the executor never

UPDATE: WHEN REIMBURSING YOURSELF FOR EXPENSES, REMEMBER THAT RESIDUARY BENEFICIARIES ARE ENTITLED TO KNOW WHAT YOU'RE SPENDING amasses unmanageable debts on behalf of the estate.

The executor should keep a receipt for every expense and know which cheque out of the estate account paid for which expenses. Don't keep track in your head; keep track on paper or computer. If he or she is claiming for mileage, it should be calculated on paper, which would then be used like a receipt (in my Alberta Probate book I provided a form for this that you can either print or download, as well as forms for all of the executor's record-keeping and accounting).

Now let me add the inevitable caveat. Be careful about what kind of thing you're claiming as an expense and don't make the mistake of thinking that everything even remotely connected to the estate is a legitimate expense. For example, flying your family members to the funeral is an individual's expense, not an estate expense. Getting that massage or that expensive champagne to manage your stress is your own expense. Remember that the residuary beneficiaries are going to examine your accounting at the end of the estate and if you have reimbursed yourself for inappropriate items, you will probably have to repay them to the estate.

Here's the second caveat. Don't be a spendthrift with estate money. The courts won't like it at all should you end up there, and that won't go well for you. Also, there might not even be enough estate funds to pay you back if the estate is small and there are debts and taxes to be paid.

What goes into an executor's accounting?

8,291 views

Many times in this blog I've mentioned that the executor accounts to the residuary beneficiaries of an estate. No doubt you have heard this mentioned elsewhere as well. If you're an executor, do you know how to prepare an accounting? If you're a beneficiary, do you know what to look for in the executor's accounts?

In this post, I'm going to talk about the basics of preparing an executor's accounting. You are most likely to see an accounting at the time that the executor is ready to distribute the estate to the beneficiaries. That means that the funeral, the bills and the taxes have all been paid, and the money left over is going to be split among the beneficiaries in accordance with the Will. The executor prepares his/her accounting, gives it to the beneficiaries, and the beneficiaries are asked to approve the accounts.

Getting the approval of the beneficiaries means that the executor is released from all personal liability for everything he/she has done. Obviously the beneficiaries are going to check everything over pretty carefully before agreeing. This post should be useful both to an executor trying to prepare accounts, and the beneficiary trying to decipher accounts.

The basic idea behind the executor's accounting is to describe what has happened with each of the assets in the estate and subtract all of the bills and liabilities that were paid out, to arrive at the present value of the estate. Here are the elements of the accounting:

1. The inventory of the estate that was included in the application for probate. This is the starting point, as the

executor is not responsible for anything that happened while the deceased was alive.

2. A Statement of receipts and disbursements. This can be either a handwritten ledger or a computer-generated statement. It shows all money that came into the estate and everything that was paid out, listed item by item, by date. Many clients find it useful to think of this statement as similar to a bank statement for the executor's bank account. Every asset that was sold - house, car, antiques, cottage - shows as money coming in. Every account or investment that is cashed in also shows as money coming in. Every bill or expense that was paid out show as outgoing money.

3. Reconciliation. Start with the value of the estate as shown on the inventory, add all incoming money, and subtract all outgoing money (using the figures on the statement of receipts and disbursements). If everything has been properly included, the number you get should be the same as the current balance in the executor's account. This, the current balance of the account, is what is now available in the estate to be divided up.

4. Statement of how much the executor wants to be paid. The amount will depend on what was said about compensation in the Will, or if nothing was said, it will depend on the guidelines for your geographical area. The amount of work and responsibility handled by the executor are also factors. The executor should state the dollar amount and how that amount was arrived at (e.g. an hourly rate, a percentage, etc.). The executor should also state how much he or she wants to be repaid for out-of-pocket expenses.

5. Statement of any money being held back for future expenses or taxes. Executors have the right to wait for a

final Tax Clearance Certificate from Canada Revenue Agency before distributing money to the beneficiaries. However, sometimes the executor agrees to distribute before the tax certificate is received. If the executor does this, he or she should figure out what the taxes might be, and what will be spent on the accountant to do the return, and keep that amount of money in the executor's account.

6. Statement of proposed distribution. The executor should state the names of the beneficiaries, the portion of the estate each will receive, and the dollar amount.

7. Release. The beneficiaries are each asked to review the accounting, and if all looks fine, to sign a release that states they are satisfied with the accounting. A wise executor won't give any beneficiaries their shares until all beneficiaries have signed releases. When all the releases are received by the executor, he or she will give the beneficiaries their cheques.

There is of course a lot more detail I could include here. (I have a chapter about this in my upcoming Alberta Probate Kit, to be released in 2011). This post is intended to give you an idea of what is involved. Executors always have the option of hiring accountants or lawyers to help them with the accounting, which is a good idea if the estate is complicated.

UPDATE: THE FORMS AND GUIDELINES FOR EXECUTOR'S ACCOUNTING IN THE ALBERTA PROBATE KIT CAN BE USED IN ALL PROVINCES.

What if a beneficiary won't sign the Release?

54,349 views

An executor emailed me recently, asking what to do if a beneficiary won't sign the Release. I don't know the facts of the case, but this appears to refer to the Release document that is given to the beneficiary for signing at the end of an estate, accompanied by financial documents that explain what the executor has done with estate assets and liabilities and how he intends to distribute the estate. If the beneficiary signs the Release, it means that he or she approves of the financial accounting provided and will not be able to come back against the executor in the future about anything covered by the accounting.

When one beneficiary doesn't sign his or her Release, it means that none of the beneficiaries can receive their inheritance.

If a beneficiary were to refuse to sign the Release, I would want to know why. Is there an objection to the contents of the financial documents? Is something missing? Does the beneficiary understand that he or she won't get any money until the accounting is approved (either by the beneficiaries or by the court)? Does the beneficiary object to the compensation the executor is requesting?

If you can find out where the objection lies, you can most likely address it. In many cases, a refusal like this is actually a request for more information. For example, say a beneficiary wants to know why the house sold for $450,000, but only $420,000 shows in the bank account. The executor could show the calculation that showed how much of the $450,000 was spent on realtor's commission, legal fees and payment of taxes. The executor could show the cancelled cheques for those expenditures. Perhaps the executor didn't do a very good job of setting out the numbers, or backing them up with receipts or statements.

Many executors who are acting without lawyers or accountants tend to give an "accounting" that is little more than the current bank balance, without explanation of what happened to investments, RRSPs, the deceased's car, etc. If that's what the executor is presenting, he or she shouldn't be surprised at the beneficiary not signing the Release. I wouldn't sign it either.

If the beneficiary is objecting to the amount of compensation that the executor is requesting, the executor might provide a breakdown of how he or she arrived at that number. The breakdown might include the number of hours the executor put in, the number of kilometers driven, or a list of all of the tasks that the executor had to take care of (this is one reason why executors are always advised to keep a diary or journal of all of their actions on behalf of an estate).

If the issue is compensation and a more detailed accounting isn't persuasive, the executor and the beneficiary may negotiate a different amount that satisfies both of them. If that doesn't work, the executor will have to ask the courts to set the

UPDATE: MEDIATION BETWEEN EXECUTOR AND BENEFICIARIES CAN BE A VERY EFFECTIVE WAY OF RESOLVING ISSUES AROUND AN EXECUTOR'S ACCOUNTING compensation by court order. This takes longer and the beneficiaries get even less because the executor's lawyer is paid from the estate, but at least the issue can be resolved.

It's unusual for a beneficiary to simply dig in his or her heels and refuse to sign the Release without giving a reason or stating an objection, but it can happen. In the end, the executor will give up on asking for information that isn't forthcoming, and will ask a judge to approve the accounting.

Taxation

Tax law is a mystery to most people, including most lawyers. It truly is a specialty practiced by accountants and a handful of math-minded lawyers. No wonder people want to read information about taxation they can actually understand. Much of what I say online about taxes is available from other sources, but nobody can understand it because it's written in secret accountant code.

I can honestly say that the questions about tax come in on my blog much faster than I can answer them. Some of them I couldn't answer supposing I had years to do so, and those are the ones I've suggested that the reader consult an accountant rather than a lawyer. I imagine that's frustrating for the reader – to wait days for an answer just to be told to ask an accountant – but it's the most appropriate answer I can give. I'm not going to guess at an answer when I know people rely on my words.

However, any estate lawyer worth her salt knows the basics of estate taxation, and that's what I share with people. Even if all I have done is alert someone to a problem, that's better than not spotting the issue and never dealing with it.

Does Canada have death taxes or inheritance taxes?

204,353 views

No, Canada does not have a specific tax that is levied against beneficiaries inheriting under an estate.

So if there is no death tax, why is there so much talk about planning ahead to pay for taxes in an estate?

There are plenty of tax consequences when a person passes away, even if there is no specific tax on dying. This is because a person's assets are deemed by law to have been disposed of by the deceased one minute before he or she died.

For example, everyone who owns an RRSP knows that we do not pay tax on the money we put into our RRSPs until we take it back out. In other words, the money is not tax-free, it is tax-deferred. Every time we take out a portion of the funds, we pay the tax on that portion. So if you were to dispose of your entire estate one minute before you died, and as part of that you took all of the money out of your RRSP (or RRIF), then you would have to pay the taxes on it.

In practice, your estate would pay those taxes, even though the person named as the beneficiary of your RRSP or RRIF is not your estate. You can avoid paying those taxes if the beneficiary you designate is your spouse or a disabled child.

Another tax liability that arises when a person passes away is capital gains tax. This is a tax on capital property (some examples of which are real estate and shares in private

66

corporations) that has increased in value since the day you acquired it.

For example, if you bought a cabin at the lake for $50,000 years ago, and by the time you die the cabin is worth $90,000, then the value of your property has gained $40,000. Half of that gain is taxable. Your executor would then have to include $20,000 (half of the gain) on your last tax return as income.

This tax is also payable out of your estate.

There is an exception to this rule as well. Your estate does not have to pay any capital gains tax on your residence. This is referred to as a capital gains exemption. If you have a home and a cabin, or a home and a rental property, you can claim the exemption only on one property, that being your usual place of residence.

There are some tools that can be used to address tax liability, such as life insurance policies, beneficiary designations, trusts and restructuring of the ownership of assets, depending on your situation.

For this reason, it's worthwhile to sit down with an experienced estate planning lawyer to make sure that you're aware of all of the possible tax consequences of your death and that of your spouse. You also want to make sure you're aware of ways to reduce taxes and to have cash flow to pay the portion that can't be reduced.

How much are Canadian inheritance taxes?
14,699 views

The intricacies of the Canadian tax system are a mystery to almost everyone. Lawyers involved in estate planning, like myself, spend quite a bit of time learning about how taxes apply to estates, and staying current with changes. So I'm not at all surprised that one of the questions I'm asked most often is about how much tax a beneficiary has to pay on an inheritance.

The answer is relatively simple for once. A beneficiary living in Canada who receives an inheritance from an estate in Canada is not taxed on the inheritance. Hooray!

This doesn't mean that taxes won't affect a beneficiary indirectly. When there are taxes to be paid by a deceased, such as capital gains tax on real estate, or income tax on an RRSP, those taxes are paid out of the estate. This means that a beneficiary who is inheriting the estate is going to inherit less because the taxes have taken a chunk.

UPDATE: EVERY PROVINCE CHARGES A COURT FEE OR PROBATE FEE FOR PROCESSING AN ESTATE. IN SOME PLACES, SUCH AS ONTARIO, IT'S REFERRED TO AS AN ESTATE TAX.

Also, the fact that something transferred tax-free to a beneficiary doesn't necessarily mean that there will never be any tax associated with that asset. For example, your mother passes away and leaves you her house. There is no capital gains tax on the transfer to you because it was her principal residence. You already have a house that you live in, so you rent it to someone for a couple of years while you decide what to do about it. Eventually you decide to sell it. If the house increases in value over that couple of years, you will have to pay the capital gain tax on the increase.

Perhaps there are no simple answers to tax questions.

Is money I get from an estate taxable?

23,857 views

I'm frequently asked this question, and I'm not surprised. Every beneficiary wants to know what the impact of a gift will be.

A general rule for estates that are administered in Canada and paid to Canadian beneficiaries is that inherited money is not taxable. So if one of your relatives leaves you $100,000 in cash in their Will, you don't have to pay tax on the $100,000.

Another general rule is that when there is a gift that gives rise to tax, the tax is paid by the estate. For example, let's look at what would happen if the $100,000 that was left to you was not held in cash, but was held in an RRSP. If you are the spouse of the deceased (or in limited circumstances, a handicapped child of the deceased), the full $100,000 of the RRSP can roll over to you without you having to pay tax at the time it's rolled to you. (The tax payment is deferred until you pass away or take the money out).

But if you are not the spouse of the deceased, then the tax situation is completely different. Everyone who has an RRSP knows that when the money goes in, it is not taxed. When it comes out, it's taxed. On estates, the law says that the deceased's RRSP is considered cashed out at the time of death. That means the tax has to be paid. Debts of an estate, including taxes, are normally paid out of the residue of an estate. For a beneficiary inheriting an RRSP this should mean that he or she gets the full value of the RRSP and the tax is paid by the estate. This assumes, of course, that there is actually enough money in the residue to pay it.

70

A similar issue arises with capital gains tax on real estate. If you inherit the house that was the deceased's principal residence, then there is no capital gains tax to worry about because a principal residence is exempt from it. But you might have been left the cottage or a revenue property or other real estate. On those properties, capital gains tax will arise. Normally this tax is paid from the residue of the estate, assuming there is cash enough to pay it.

UPDATE: WHEN A BENEFICIARY RECEIVES THE FULL AMOUNT OF AN RRSP OR RRIF AND THERE IS NOT ENOUGH MONEY IN THE ESTATE TO PAY THE TAXES ON THAT FUND, CANADA REVENUE AGENCY MAY PURSUE THE BENEFICIARY FOR THE UNPAID TAX.

Keep in mind that in particular circumstances, the beneficiary could still be affected by tax arising from the gift. The wording of a Will can make a big difference. In some Wills, the deceased has stated that each person who inherits something under the Will will pay the tax on his or her own inheritance, instead of the estate paying it. That is perfectly legal.

Another important note about estate money is that the fees taken by an executor for his or her work on the estate are taxable. They must be included as earned income on the executor's personal income tax return.

Estate taxes are tricky. Executors should be careful and consult accountants or estate lawyers if things get complicated.

Is there capital gains tax when I sell an inherited property?

55,993 views

The following is a question I received from a reader. It's a variation on a question that I hear a lot, so I thought I'd address it here. Just a caveat - when you ask me questions here on this blog, I don't get to know the whole picture, so my answers are necessarily general. You should always back up this information by talking to a lawyer or accountant in person.

"My father died this past November and left everything to myself and sister, including his house/property. If we sell this property this summer, do we have to claim a capital gains? If so, on what part?"

On the transfer of the property from you to a third party, you are probably going to be liable for capital gains tax. The period that you're on the hook for is from the date you acquire it to the day you sell it. Since this period of time will be only a matter of months, the property might not incur too much of a

UPDATE: REMEMBER THAT IT'S NOT A HOUSE THAT IS TAX-EXEMPT, IT'S A SPECIFIC TRANSACTION. IF YOU SELL A HOUSE THAT IS NOT YOUR PRINCIPAL RESIDENCE, IN TERMS OF TAXATION IT DOESN'T MATTER WHETHER YOU BOUGHT IT YOURSELF OR INHERITED IT.

gain in that time, and therefore your tax will be small. You and your sister can split the tax between you as you are both inheriting the property.

Note that if the property in question is your principal residence (which doesn't seem to be the case here), the tax is not payable on your sale of it, because this is an exception to the general rule of capital gains.

Now let's look at the first transfer - that of the property from your father to you. Since you describe it as "house/property" rather than just "house", I'm assuming there is something more than just a house. When these items transfer to you, there is no tax for you personally to pay. However, there certainly may be taxes that must be paid by the estate.

When your father passed away, there would have been no capital gains tax payable on his home (principal residence). Note that only 3 acres of property can be included in the principal residence exemption. If there was an additional property, such as a cottage or revenue property, there is capital gains tax payable on that property. Keep in mind that if the property sits in the name of the estate for a long time, there may also be tax payable on the increase in value while it's in the estate name.

As you can see, it seems a simple question but the answer is complicated. This is why I recommend that you sit down with an accountant to figure out the tax details.

Should I add my child's name to the title of my house to avoid tax in the future?

32,341 views

An awful lot of parents have added their children to the title of their homes without getting legal or accounting advice first. In fact, I'm amazed at how many people have done this, given the risks and complications. A reader wrote to me to ask about whether he should add his oldest daughter to his house title. I suggest that anyone who is considering making this move, or has already done so, should read this post for some food for thought. His question and my reply are below:

> *"I am in the middle of purchasing a residential property. Is there any advantage if I purchase in my name + wife's name and eldest daughter's name. My thinking is for future when we both are not here, then our daughter retains this property without any tax implications."*

When considering putting extra names on a title, it's a mistake to focus on just one aspect of the transaction, whether that aspect is tax, probate avoidance or any other concern. You have to look at the bigger picture.

You have to realize that in adding your daughter's name to your home, you are creating a huge risk to yourself. There are a dozen ways in which this could cause you to lose your home, or to lose a substantial sum of money to hold onto your home. If your daughter were to get divorced, her spouse could claim half the value of the house and if she doesn't have the funds to pay this out, you could end up paying it yourself just to stay in your own home.

75

If you are like most parents, you will stubbornly believe that your daughter will never do anything that would negatively impact you. As a parent, I understand that faith, but as an estate lawyer I know how misplaced it is. There are things that could happen to your daughter accidentally that could cause you to lose your home. For example, if she is sued because of a car accident or if she declares bankruptcy or if she has a business failure for which she has provided a personal guarantee, you could lose your home. It's impossible to say at this moment that none of these things will happen during your lifetime.

You also need to look more closely at your presumption that your daughter will "retain this property". It sounds as if you have more than one child. If you have a will that leaves your estate equally among your children, you have to ensure that you are clear about whether this house is part of her share. Otherwise it could lead to a dispute among the children.

You may run into the issue of inter-generational joint property. From what you've said, your intention is not for her to own the property but simply to avoid tax issues.

UPDATE: THE FACT THAT ADDING A NAME TO A HOUSE TITLE IS SO EASY REALLY MISLEADS A LOT OF PEOPLE. IT'S EASY TO GET INTO, BUT DIFFICULT AND EXPENSIVE TO GET OUT OF LATER.

Therefore it isn't a "true" joint ownership in the sense that you don't intend for her to own and retain this property for her own use after your death. Your property may be held in trust for the estate until a judge decides on the available evidence whether or not this is a true joint ownership.

Now, to your question about tax implications. If the residential property was owned just by you and your wife, and it was your principal residence, there would be no tax anyway when the property was sold or transferred on your death. So you aren't avoiding any tax by adding your daughter's name.

If it's not your principal residence but is a second property such as a cabin, revenue property or simply a second family home, then there is going to be capital gains tax on its sale or transfer (assuming that it increases in value) even if your daughter's name is on it.

Let's say that your daughter is single now but gets married, and she and her husband buy a home. You may one day decide to sell your house either because you want to move somewhere else or because you are going to live in a care facility. As your house won't be her principal residence, her share of the transaction will be taxable.

The best people to talk to about taxes are accountants. If you have a chance to discuss this transaction with an accountant, I think that would be a good idea.

The basics of capital gains tax and the principal residence
82,003 views

As I've mentioned several times in previous blog posts, Canada doesn't currently have any direct death or inheritance federal taxes. But when a person passes away, his or her estate must pay income tax outstanding as well as capital gains tax.

Capital gains tax is the tax paid on the increase in value of certain assets known as capital property. The type of capital property dealt with by executors most often is real estate, though other assets such as the shares of a privately-owned corporation are also capital property.

Capital gains tax works like this. On the day you first acquire an asset, it has a value (called the adjusted cost base). If we are dealing with real estate, the value is normally the price you paid for the property. Over the time that you own that property, it gains in value. The longer you own it, the more likely that the value will increase. On the day you get rid of the asset - by selling it or transferring it under your Will when you die - it therefore has a greater value than it did when you got it. The difference between the value on the day you got it and the value on the day you dispose of it is known as the capital gain. You have to pay tax on one-half of that increase in value.

As an example, let's say Leia buys a house for $150,000. She owns it for many years and when she dies, her executor is going to sell the house. Now it's worth $550,000. The capital gain on the property is $400,000. Leia's estate has to pay tax on half, or $200,000. This doesn't mean that there is $200,000 in tax owing. It means that $200,000 is added to income for that year on the tax return, and the executor will use as many tax deductions, exemptions etc. as he or she can to reduce how much tax must be paid.

If the property was worth less at the date of her death than it was when Leia acquired it, she would instead have a capital loss that she could apply to her return.

This is triggered by Leia's death because in law you are deemed to have sold everything you own one minute before you died. This means that even if your executor is not selling the house but is transferring it to a beneficiary, you are still deemed in law to have sold it at fair market value.

There are some exemptions to the rule about capital gains. The one that is important to most executors is that a person does not have to pay capital gains tax when he or she disposes of his or her principal residence. So if the house Leia owned was her principal residence, the $200,000 would not have to be added to her income.

On the other hand, if the house Leia owned was a summer cottage or a rental property, the tax would be owing.

Your principal residence doesn't necessarily have to be the house you live in most of the time. If you happen to own another house that is worth more, you could designate that more expensive one as your principal residence (don't do this without talking it over with your accountant first!).

A married couple only gets one principal residence between them.

Before taking any steps to avoid capital gains tax by setting up trusts or joint ownership or other ideas, you absolutely must speak with an accountant or estate planning specialist about your specific situation. Often people set up schemes to avoid one thing but they haven't looked at the whole tax picture, such as potential tax hits when a property is transferred from an individual to a trust or to joint owners. There may also be other tax solutions available that you hadn't thought of.

UPDATE: A COMMON MISTAKE IS TO BELIEVE THAT A HOUSE YOU LIVE IN IS A PRINCIPAL RESIDENCE SIMPLY BECAUSE YOU HAVE LIVED THERE FOR A LONG TIME. HOWEVER, IF YOU DO NOT OWN THE PROPERTY YOURSELF, IT CANNOT BE A PRINCIPAL RESIDENCE FOR TAX EXEMPTION PURPOSES.

Income tax returns that an executor must file

22,112 views

The executor of the estate of a deceased person is responsible for filing tax returns on behalf of the deceased person and also on behalf of the estate. I once had a client who was the executor of an estate who asked a professional tax preparer to prepare the return for the estate and was told that "you can't file a tax return for a dead person" and was turned away. The tax preparer was simply wrong. You can, and must, file certain returns on behalf of a deceased individual.

These are the returns that are required to be filed on the death of a person for whom you are the executor:

1. T1 Terminal Return for the year of death. This is a personal tax return for the person who died, as opposed to his or her estate. It will cover the period starting on January 1 of the year of death and ending on the date of death. For example, if the person died on March 15, 2010, the return would cover the period of January 1, 2010 to March 15, 2010. This return is due on the later of either

- a) the normal filing deadline of April 30 of the year of death, or

- b) b) six months after death.

2. Any T1 Returns for the deceased person for previous years that the deceased has not filed. They are due six months after death, but since they are already late and therefore subject to penalties and interest, it is best to get them filed as soon as possible.

3. Rights or Things Return. This return does not apply to every estate. It is a return that is filed when there were amounts due to the deceased person which were not paid to him or her yet at the date of death, and therefore were not included in the last T1 return. Examples of the amounts are unpaid work-in-progress for a professional person, dividends that were declared but paid, and farm crops that were not yet harvested.

This return is due on the later of either

a) one year after death, or

b) 90 days after assessment of the T1 Terminal Return.

Your best bet is to hire an accountant or tax preparer who has experience with estate returns. Not all accountants do the same kind of work, so look for someone whose experience is in taxation or estates.

If you'd like to read more about taxation of estates (and hey, who wouldn't?) check out a paper I wrote for the Legal Education Society in 2009 called Taxation of the Average Estate.

Should an executor get a tax clearance certificate?

17,613 views

Clearance certificates are written notices from Canada Revenue Agency that state that taxes owing, and any interest and penalties on those taxes, have been paid by an estate. This is important because if an executor should distribute the assets of an estate before getting a clearance certificate, and not all taxes have been paid, the executor can be personally liable for payment of the taxes out of his or her own pocket.

The final clearance certificate absolves the executor from that liability. I refer to "final" certificate here because it is also possible to get interim certificates if you are working on a lengthy or complicated estate.

To get a clearance certificate you have to apply for it, because it will not automatically be issued. Usually the accountant who prepares the income tax returns for the estate will send in the application along with the final tax return. You do have to specifically ask the accountant to do this, so if he or she doesn't bring it up for some reason, you should bring it up yourself. If you have a lawyer helping you with the estate, do not expect that the lawyer will apply for this because it's an accounting function.

There is a long wait to receive the clearance certificate once you have applied for it. Allow six months for this. Usually beneficiaries of an estate are unhappy about waiting an additional six months to receive their inheritance, even though they are told that the executor must hold onto at least enough of the estate to pay upcoming taxes. In a future post I'll talk about how to distribute the bulk of the estate while waiting for the clearance certificate.

It isn't required by law that an executor get a clearance certificate. However, if you're an executor, it's certainly a good idea to have that confirmation in your hand that you are no longer personally at risk for payment of estate taxes.

How do I get a Tax Clearance Certificate?
22,178 views

A tax clearance certificate is a notice you receive from Canada Revenue Agency that states that all taxes owing on an estate have been paid. Although it is not the law that every executor must get one, the majority of executors will do so. This is because if the executor goes ahead and distributes the estate to the beneficiaries and then later finds out that there is tax owing, the executor himself might have to pay the taxes out of his own money.

I'm often asked how a person goes about getting a tax clearance certificate. The certificate does not come out automatically; it has to be requested in the right way at the right time. The vast majority of executors that I've worked with have asked the accountant who does the tax returns for the estate to request the clearance certificate. This is because accountants who are familiar with taxation know how and when to get it.

However, if you want to request one yourself, here are the basic steps:

- file all of the necessary tax returns for the deceased and the estate;

- receive the Notice of Assessment for the returns you've filed;

- fill in a form called TX19, that you can find online here;

- send the form to your local tax office, along with a copy of the Will, a copy of all probate documents and a statement of proposed distribution.

- wait.

It takes a long time to get the tax clearance certificate. You should expect to wait several months in most cases. Because of the long wait and the unwillingness of beneficiaries to wait longer than necessary for their inheritance, there is a process in place for making an interim distribution of the bulk of the estate while keeping back enough money to pay the taxes and future expenses. I'll post about that interim process in a separate post.

To go to the Canada Revenue Agency page on clearance certificates, [link removed during editing].

Can an executor distribute estate assets before getting the tax clearance certificate?
131,658 views

As I mentioned in a recent post about tax clearance certificates, an executor is entitled to wait for Canada Revenue Agency to send him or her a Tax Clearance Certificate before giving the beneficiaries their shares of the estate. This procedure arises from the fact that an executor is required by law to pay all debts and taxes before giving money to beneficiaries, and the Clearance Certificate is proof that there are no more taxes owing by the estate.

However, there is a process for an executor to give the beneficiaries most of their inheritance before getting the Clearance Certificate, a process known as an *interim distribution*.

Before an executor takes this step, consider the fact that if he or she pays the beneficiaries before paying Canada Revenue Agency, that executor will have to come up with the tax money, even if it is out of his or her own money. Once you've given the money out to the beneficiaries, it's pretty hard to get some of it back again to pay taxes.

To boil down a detailed process into a simple description, the idea of an interim distribution is to hold back enough money in the estate to pay future taxes, future expenses and any legal or accounting fees, and to distribute the rest to the beneficiaries. The executor will produce a legal accounting of the estate that details all of his or her financial transactions on behalf of the estate. It will also include a Statement of Proposed Distribution that shows how much of the estate the executor proposes to give out to the beneficiaries now, and how much is being held back for taxes and other expenses. The financial documents are given to the beneficiaries along with a Release document. If all beneficiaries agree and sign their Releases, then the executor can go ahead with the interim distribution.

How do you know how much to hold back for taxes? Obviously you must get this number correct. I have never proceeded with an interim distribution without working with a tax accountant who can estimate better than I can what taxes might be owing by the estate.

Most of the time, beneficiaries will pressure executors to make an interim distribution because it takes months to get a Tax Clearance Certificate. However, beneficiaries should understand that they cannot force an executor to make an interim distribution because it means the executor is assuming risk for the payment of estate taxes.

What is a T3 tax return?
5,373 views

When a person passes away, his or her executor files a tax return for the last year of the deceased's life. That is a T1 tax return. Executors are sometimes surprised to find that they may have to file a tax return for the estate itself, as opposed to for the deceased person. A tax return for an estate or trust is a T3 return.

An estate or trust is considered a "person" for taxation purposes. Just as a living person files a tax return each year to report income, so does an estate or trust.

An estate's tax year begins the day after a person passes away and continues for one year. Any income earned by the estate during the tax year is reported on a T3 return, and is set off against available deductions and exemptions just as it is for a living person. Income earned by an estate may be in the form of capital gain, dividends or interest. If an estate doesn't earn any income, it may not be necessary to file a T3 return.

If an estate carries on for many years, a T3 return has to be filed for each year. When the estate is wound up and all of its assets have been distributed to the beneficiaries, the executor should request a Tax Clearance Certificate from Canada Revenue Agency to show that all taxes owing have been paid.

I always advise my clients to consult an accountant to help with tax returns for an estate. While lawyers such as myself know the basics of estate tax returns, we are not qualified to complete the returns, and an executor should enlist the help of an accountant for that. Accountants can also give advice on whether tax owing on income earned by an estate or trust can be shared out among the beneficiaries rather than borne by the trust itself.

What does "deemed disposition on death" mean?

4,272 views

If you've ever heard an estate-planning presentation or read an article about it, you've no doubt heard of the "deemed disposition on death". This brief phrase has enormous implications for every estate, so it's important to understand what it means and how it affects your estate planning.

The phrase means that everything you own (house, investments, shares in a business, RRSP, vehicles, you name it) is deemed to have been sold or cashed in by you one minute before you died. Deemed by who, you ask? By Canada Revenue Agency and the various laws of Wills.

Since you didn't actually liquidate everything immediately before passing away, it is only deemed to have happened, and we all have to behave as if it did.

The major impact this will have on your estate has to do with taxation. The deemed disposition will trigger the payment of income tax on any assets that you are holding on a tax-deferred basis. For example, the money you've put into your RRSP has not yet been taxed. Taxes are deferred until you take the money back out. If you cashed it in right before you passed away then you've taken the money out and you have to pay all of the tax on it. Since you have passed away, your estate has to pay it.

Deemed disposition of other assets also triggers capital gains and capital losses. For example, if you own a cottage or a rental property, you are deemed to have sold it at fair market value right before you passed away. The difference in value from the time you acquired it to the date you disposed of it is called the capital gain (if it increased in

91

value) or a capital loss (if it decreased in value). If there is a gain, half of the gain is taxable and again, your estate will have to pay that. Note that capital gains do NOT apply to your principal residence.

The end result of all of this tax treatment is that sometimes estates end up with less cash than the deceased person thought he or she would have. It's not at all uncommon for people who don't go through lawyers or financial planners to forget to take taxation into account. This can mean very unfair divisions of estates even though the testator had intended an equal split.

Wills, probate, and intestacy

The posts in this section answer questions people ask before they get to the estate administration side of things. These are the questions they ask as they set up their own wills. They want to know the best way to do things and what things cost. Many of the posts I make under this heading are inspired directly by questions I'm asked every single day at work and online.

The questions I receive about wills lead me to conclude that some of the people asking the questions have already decided what they want to do, and they are simply seeking confirmation that they can actually do it. All they really want is a yes-or-no answer. Preferably a yes.

A point that I've tried to make to readers several times is that they are asking the wrong questions. They ask "can I name so-and-so as my executor" and "can I do my will without a lawyer" when those questions should really start with *should I,* not *can I*. It's not just semantics; it's a hugely important difference.

In seminars, I give examples of things that people can do but should not do, and the audience members get it. It's harder online to judge whether people actually receive that message. So at the risk of repeating myself, I urge readers to think about *should I* rather than *can I*.

Can my executor also be a beneficiary?

11,758 views

I am often asked by people planning their Wills whether it is possible for a beneficiary under their Will to also be named as the executor. This is particularly common in family situations when of course people want to name their own spouses and children as both beneficiary and executor.

UPDATE: ALTHOUGH THIS POST MENTIONS ALBERTA, THE RULE IS THE SAME RIGHT ACROSS THE COUNTRY

In Alberta there is no law that excludes someone from being both beneficiary and executor. This is done all the time, for example where a married couple name each other as their executors and also leave their estates to each other. In cases like that, not only is there no prohibition against the arrangement, but it is clearly the best arrangement that could be made for that particular person's Will. When one person is inheriting the whole estate, having that person act as executor can simplify administrative matters.

There are some situations in which it does not always make sense for the beneficiary and the executor to be the same person. For example, if you are setting up a trust for your son that is intended to ensure that the son doesn't blow all of his money, it doesn't really make sense for the son to be the executor (which also makes him the trustee of his own trust). When the executor is also the trustee of a trust, he or

94

she usually has the power to decide how much of the money in trust is paid to the beneficiary at any given time. It isn't much protection to put the son in charge of deciding how much money he is to receive.

Rather than naming the first person who comes to mind as your executor, put some thought into what an executor under your Will is going to have to do once you have passed away. Once you have an idea what the challenges will be, you can better decide who is equipped to handle those challenges. Remember that if you need a neutral third party to handle a trust, though not necessarily the whole executorship, you can always consider naming a trust company.

There is one restriction that can cause a problem. You cannot allow your beneficiaries to also act as witnesses. Should one of your beneficiaries also be a witness, your Will is still valid, but that beneficiary's gift is invalid. I have seen Wills in which the person had his children act as witnesses to his home-made Will, and tried to leave the estate to those same children. The gifts were invalid, which basically left the man with no Will at all. Fortunately the mistake was discovered on a Will review while the man was still alive and able to correct it.

Can I appoint my lawyer as my executor?

7,398 views

In Canada, you can appoint either an individual or a trust company as your executor. If the individual you choose is a lawyer, that's the same as appointing any other person. It means, however, that you can't appoint the law firm that the lawyer works for, just the lawyer himself or herself.

By the way, I should clear up one common misconception here. If your lawyer acts as your executor, your lawyer cannot charge your estate for executor work at the same rate he or she would charge for legal work. Your lawyer may charge $350 to work on your lawsuit or contract, but he or she cannot charge that much for executor work. This is because you appointed an individual executor who just happens to be a lawyer. The lawyer will be limited to charging what any other executor could charge (in Canada, that's 1% to 5% of the estate).

If your executor is a lawyer and he or she does legal work for the estate, such as applying for probate, then that work can be charged at full lawyer's rates, because your executor would have to pay a lawyer for that anyway.

In my years of private practice, before coming to my current job of in-house lawyer, I was asked many, many times to act as executor for clients. I almost always turned it down. In speaking with other lawyers about this, I understand that most lawyers will turn it down most of the time. Where your lawyer is a family member or close friend, that's different. However, I think that even if you do want to appoint your lawyer, you may not be able to get your lawyer to agree to it.

Most people will ask their lawyer to be their executor because they don't have anyone in the family or a close friend that they feel is appropriate. This often happens when people have immigrated to Canada from another country and don't have relatives in Canada. It also happens when people don't have children, or their children live far away, or perhaps don't get along. It can also happen when the clients want to set up lengthy or complicated trusts that they don't feel would be best managed by an inexperienced person.

Before you name your lawyer as your executor, think about this. If you name your lawyer as your executor, and your lawyer dies before your estate or your trusts are wound up, who is then in charge of your estate? The executor named in your lawyer's Will becomes your executor. Do you even know who that is? Your lawyer's husband/wife? One of the lawyer's children? Remember that you are appointing the individual person who happens to be a lawyer; you're not appointing the law firm.

The same idea applies when you appoint your accountant, your financial planner or your doctor, all of whom I hear proposed as possible executors from time to time.

UPDATE: IF YOU NAME AN INDIVIDUAL AS YOUR EXECUTOR, YOU SHOULD ALWAYS NAME AN ALTERNATE WHO CAN TAKE OVER IF YOUR FIRST NAMED EXECUTOR CANNOT FINISH THE JOB

If you don't have an appropriate family member, or

you need specialized skills for your estate that you are not
sure are available in your family, consider a trust company.
Most people immediately think that using a trust company
is terribly expensive, but in reality it's cheaper than you
think. It's certainly worth a phone call to a trust company,
or a conversation with your banker, to find out what it
would cost you. And always remember to look at the value
of what you're getting and not just the price of what you're
getting.

How do I change executors?
8,760 views

I'm often asked this question, but before answering I always ask whether the person's whose Will it is (the testator) is still alive. In other words, are you trying to change the appointment of an executor in a Will, or are you trying to change an executor who is already in charge of an estate?

A person can change his or her choice of executor in the Will as long as he or she has mental capacity to do so. Changing the executor doesn't necessarily mean making a whole new Will. If you are happy with your Will other than the executor you have named, you can have a Codicil made that only changes the executorship. A Codicil is simply a new, brief document that amends your Will. It is much like a Will, in that all of the rules for Will-making also apply to Codicils. The advantage to having a Codicil made is that the process and the document are shorter and less expensive.

The Will and the Codicil must be kept together so that they can be read as one document.

If you are interested in changing an executor who was named in the Will but who has not done anything on behalf of the estate, and who doesn't want to do anything for the estate, that executor can opt out. The legal term for it is *renouncing* the right to be an executor. An executor might renounce if he or she is too ill to be the executor, if he or she has moved very far away, if he or she has lost mental capacity, if he or she doesn't get along with the family members, or for other reasons.

The important thing to remember about renouncing is that it can only be done right at the beginning of an estate before an executor does any work. Once the executor takes any steps at all as executor, he or she can't quit being an executor until the court says so.

If an executor renounces and there is an alternate executor named, the alternate executor can then take over and be in charge of the estate.

If there is no alternate executor named, you are left with a Will that is completely valid except that there is no executor to carry out the work. At this point, someone will have to be appointed as an administrator of the estate. The Will is still used, but the court will appoint an administrator to do the work that the executor would have done.

If an executor is part way through the job of being an executor and wants to resign from it, he or she must ask the court for permission. At that time, the executor will be required to give a full accounting of all financial transactions that he or she has done on behalf of the estate. This includes an update on the current balances and values of all accounts, properties and other assets, and an explanation for each expenditure. This process is sometimes called passing of accounts. Until the court has approved the accounts and dismissed the executor, he or she remains the executor.

Sometimes the family members want to change or remove an executor who they believe is not doing a good job. They want to remove someone who doesn't want to be removed. This is not easy. The court will not want to remove an executor who was chosen personally by the executor without very good reason. It is pretty nasty litigation most of the time, and not something that should be attempted lightly.

What happens if my executor lives outside the province?

11,309 views

This is a very common question, given how families these days are spread out all over the country and perhaps even beyond. If you've appointed someone outside the province as your executor, you need to be aware of the rules about that. Although I am quoting Alberta legislation in this post, other provinces also have similar rules.

If the executor you've named in your Will lives outside of Alberta, the Surrogate Rules of Court which govern estate and probate matters say that before your executor may take control of your estate, he or she must post a bond. The bond is to be for the full amount of your estate. The point of the bond is to provide some assurance that the creditors and beneficiaries of the estate will be paid before the executor leaves the province.

So, if this is your situation, what can you do? There are solutions available.

A popular idea is to appoint co-executors, with one being your out-of-province executor and the other

UPDATE: THE REQUIREMENT THAT AN OUT-OF-PROVINCE EXECUTOR MUST OBTAIN A BOND IS NOT LIMITED TO ALBERTA. IT IS REQUIRED IN OTHER (BUT NOT ALL) PROVINCES AS SWELL.

living in Alberta. This refers to two (or more) executors who must work jointly to administer your estate. As long as one of the executors lives in Alberta, you will not have to post a bond.

Another good idea is to appoint a trust company, which is resident in almost every province and territory in Canada. The trust company can act alone as your executor, or can be a co-executor with someone else.

If you've been putting off getting your Will made because you're stuck on the question of who to appoint as your executor, a better idea is to sit down with an estate-planning lawyer and ask for ideas. You just might hear something that works for you.

How many executors should I have?

3,157 views

The executor named in your Will is the person who is going to take charge of all aspects of your legal and financial affairs after you have passed away. Your executor is going to have a lot of authority, so the proper choice of executor is crucial.

Some people like the idea of having more than one executor, which is an option. Sometimes this is because there is a lot of work to be done. For example, the owner of a large business might want to have someone familiar with his business to act together with someone from his family. The goal there is to share the workload and pool the skills and knowledge of the two executors.

Sometimes people want more than one executor because they hope the executors will keep an eye on each other and keep each other honest.

If there is more than one executor named, the co-executors must act jointly. Neither of them is the "lead" executor or "main" executor. Each has equal legal authority. If you are considering naming more than one person to act as your executor, give some thought to how well the two (or more) of them will get along. How difficult will it be for them to reach important decisions together?

From time to time I hear from clients who want to appoint all of their children together to be their executors. As a general rule, I'm not in favour of that because I don't think it's realistic. For one thing, if four or five people have to review and sign every document, everything is going to take longer. For another thing, the chances that four or five siblings will agree on the myriad of decisions that have to be made on an estate are next to nothing. People have different values, different expectations, different decision-making styles, and of course each of them has a spouse with an opinion as well. In my experience, this is asking too much of people, particularly at a time when emotions are close to the surface and everyone is dealing with the loss of a loved one.

Having three executors is relatively rare, but does happen particularly for business owners. In this case, be sure to consider putting in a clause that allows decisions to be made by majority vote rather than unanimity, to avoid deadlocks.

If you are appointing just one person as your executor, as most people do, you must also appoint an alternate executor. The alternate does not work with the executor. The alternate only comes into the picture if the first-named executor is unable or unwilling to take on the job. In older Wills, the alternate could only take over as executor if the first-named executor had died. In more modern Wills, the alternate can also be called upon to take over if the first-named executor has lost mental capacity or simply refuses to act as executor.

Often husbands and wives name each other as their executor but aren't sure who to appoint to act when both of them have passed away. A solution that is becoming more popular is naming a trust company to do the bulk of the work, together with one of the children.

Do not choose anyone to be your executor simply because you want to do them an honour. Being an executor is hard work. Generally executors don't enjoy it. Try to choose an executor based on who is best suited to do the work you need them to do. Consider geographical distance. Consider personalities and personal skills. And of course, you must consider trustworthiness.

Who can witness a Will?

14,374 views

It's easy to make mistakes when you're making legal documents without a lawyer, and witnessing is certainly an area that causes problems. To be fair, I have once or twice seen lawyers make mistakes with witnessing too!

Who can witness a person signing his or her Will or Codicil? Pretty much anyone who has reached the age of majority and is mentally competent can be a witness, but there are some exceptions.

No beneficiary of your Will should be a witness to that Will. Neither should that beneficiary's spouse or common-law spouse be a witness. If they do act as a witness, the gift you want to leave to that beneficiary becomes invalid. Not only would that disappoint the beneficiary, but it could also leave you partially intestate (i.e. some assets not covered by the Will).

It is perfectly alright for your executor to be a witness. However, that won't work if the executor is also a beneficiary, as mentioned in the previous paragraph. If the executor acts as a witness, he or she might also be endangering his or her chance of being paid for acting as your executor.

It is alright for a creditor of the deceased to be a witness.

When I'm visiting a person at their home or at a care facility to have a Will signed, it isn't always possible for me to bring witnesses along. In a case like that, neighbours or staff at the care facility can act as witnesses. To protect my client's privacy, I do not ask the neighbours or the staff to

107

read the document, though I make it clear that it is a Will that is being signed.

A Will has to be signed by the testator in front of two witnesses who both watch him or her sign. Then the witnesses both sign in front of the testator and each other. Later, one of the witnesses must sign an Affidavit stating that all of the proper formalities of Will signing were followed.

A holograph Will that is 100% in your own handwriting does not need to be witnessed (make sure you date it and sign it though).

UPDATE: PROVINCES WHICH ALLOW HOLOGRAPHIC WILLS ARE ALBERTA, MANITOBA, NEW BRUNSWICK, NEWFOUNDLAND AND LABRADOR, ONTARIO, QUEBEC, AND SASKATCHEWAN.

Should I designate a person or my estate as beneficiary?
6,012 views

You readers come up with great questions for me, there's no doubt about that. And I do my best to answer as many as I can. Here's one about beneficiaries that I know many people would like to know more about.

The question:

> *"It would seem to me that naming a person as a beneficiary instead of an estate would be the easiest and fastest route for distribution. Is there some benefit that I can't see to naming an "estate" as a beneficiary?"*

There are some very good reasons for naming your estate as beneficiary rather than an individual person. But it all depends on what the asset is, who the person is, and the estate set-up as a whole. In other words, there is no one right answer for everyone and you have to figure it out differently for each person. But here are some things you may not have thought of:

Let's look first at RRSPs and RRIFs. If you have a spouse, you will probably name your spouse as beneficiary to take advantage of the tax rollover. But if you don't have a spouse, who do you name? Many people at that point name "all my kids". In a lot of cases, they might be better off naming the estate. For one thing, there is no tax advantage to naming your children because there is no tax rollover (except in certain circumstances where the child is handicapped). Secondly, most people leave their estates to their children, and say that if the child has predeceased, the child's children get the child's share. This won't happen to money in an RRSP if a child predeceases you. It will be split among the remaining named children and none will go to your deceased child's children.

Also, if you leave your RRSP to one of your children, that child will get the full RRSP value and the tax on it will be paid by whoever is inheriting the rest of your estate, presumably your other children.

Now let's look at real estate. Having your spouse on the title to your home so that they inherit the home makes perfect sense in the majority of cases. However, many people do what they think of as estate planning by putting one or more of their children's names on their homes and cottages so that there is no need to go through probate. I can't even begin to describe the number of ways in which this backfires. Confusion, delays, lawsuits, tax issues, and fights between siblings - all of this and more happens when you try to bypass probate this way. It's such a bad idea I can't believe anyone still does it.

Next, life insurance. There are plenty of good reasons to name individual beneficiaries of life insurance policies, and I don't argue with any of them. However, sometimes there are reasons to name your estate to receive the life insurance funds. One of the main purposes is to create some cash in your estate to pay for taxes. Having money for taxes could be the difference between having to sell something important, such as the family cottage, and keeping it. Having cash in the estate will pay for funeral expenses, pay off debts and allow all beneficiaries to receive a larger inheritance.

Also keep in mind that when you leave life insurance or RRSP to a child, they will inherit it all when they reach age of majority. You may or may not think that that's a suitable age for someone to receive a large sum of money.

As you can see, there are many ways for a person to deal with any particular asset. Sometimes naming an individual as the beneficiary of an asset is exactly the way to go, and sometimes it's not. The best way to get advice about this is to sit down with an estate planning lawyer and look at that asset together with all the rest of your assets in the context of your family and your goals. Make sure it all works together.

Using a will kit: do you need the Affidavit of Witness?

5,929 views

If you have used a will kit, or are thinking about using one, please read this reader's question and my answer. It's very easy to make a mistake when preparing your own will, and ignoring instructions in the will kit isn't going to help.

> *"My husband and I recently did our wills through an online will kit. Do you think it's a necessary step for the witnesses to sign an Affidavit of a Witness to a Will?"*

Yes, I do think it's a necessary step. Why would you choose to skip a step that the kit tells you to complete?

Assuming that you have made your will correctly and have had it witnessed correctly (two very big leaps of faith for online will kits, but that's a story for another day), then your will is valid without the Affidavit of Witness being attached. However, your will can't be probated without the Affidavit, so leaving off the Affidavit is a mistake.

When a will is sent to the court for probate, the court needs proof that the will was properly signed and witnessed. By "properly" I'm referring not just to the fact that each page was initialled and the last one was signed, but also to issues such as the person signing being of the age of majority and being of sound mind. This proof is provided by the Affidavit of Witness.

If you don't have it signed now, once you pass away your executor will have to find one of the witnesses and have it signed. This won't necessarily be easy, as witnesses may move away or lose touch with you. Or they may pass away.

Why cause this kind of problem when you can prevent it by having the Affidavit signed now?

It makes me nervous that you are questioning parts of the instructions provided to you for setting up a proper will. You may be skipping over information or steps that are vitally important to a valid document. Please do not make the mistake of assuming that you don't need the Affidavit because your will won't need to be probated. You can't know that ahead of time.

My experience has been that some people mis-use will kits. They don't want to bother getting advice or paying a lawyer so they willfully ignore potential issues and problems. Those are the people whose families pay for it later. You can produce a valid will using a will kit, but only if you have followed all of the instructions provided by the kit, including the advice about getting the Affidavit signed.

What do lawyers charge to make Wills?

14,307 views

In their June 2010 edition, Canadian Lawyer magazine has presented the results of a survey of law firms across Canada to find out what lawyers are charging clients to prepare their documents. While the survey covers several kinds of fees from criminal defense work to intellectual property, I'm going to focus just on the fees for Wills and Powers of Attorney (in other words I'm picking and choosing from the data). The link to the digital edition of the magazine is here, but you will need an email address to access it so I'm not sure if everyone can actually see the article.

Ontario:
- fees to do a simple will range from $278 to $510
- fees to do a complex will range from $704 to $2,061
- fees to do a power of attorney range from $108 to $219

Western Canada:
- fees to do a simple will range from $242 to $508
- fees to do a complex will range from $538 to $1,520
- fees to do a power of attorney range from $124 to $251

Atlantic Canada and Quebec:
- fees to do a simple will range from $215 to $642
- fees to do a complex will range from $662 to $2,100
- fees to do a power of attorney range from $137 to $338

It's also interesting to compare the average cost nationally by the size of the law firm:

- simple will by a firm having 1-4 lawyers: average $294
- simple will by a firm having 5-25 lawyers: average $413
- simple will by a firm having 26+ lawyers: average $489

- complex will by a firm having 1-4 lawyers: average $751
- complex will by a firm having 5-25 lawyers: average $1,147
- complex will by a firm having 26+ lawyers: average $1,520

I still sometimes hear people, who apparently have sticker shock when they are quoted a price by a lawyer, saying things like "I can get a Will from the lawyer down the street for $100". Seriously, the days of $100 Wills are over. You might as well do it yourself as pay the person who charges $100. The real value of a lawyer when preparing your Will is the advice that you get on trusts, taxes and executorship, and the peace of mind that your family is protected.

Can't I just use a codicil instead of a whole new will?

5,221 views

A Codicil is an amendment to an existing Will. It's much like a mini-Will, because it has a similar format and has all the same signing/witnessing requirements as a Will. A Codicil is shorter than a Will (rarely running more than one page long) and is quicker and cheaper to prepare than a new Will.

The problem with saying that something is cheaper is that to many people, cheaper is always better. Codicils, like everything else, are useful in the right circumstances. When you need a new Will but all you're prepared to pay for is a Codicil, you're not getting the right document.

A Codicil is intended to make a small change to your Will that doesn't affect the overall structure of your estate plan. For example, if you have appointed your brother as your executor then he moves to Australia, you might not want to have someone that far away to look after your estate. To change your choice of executors, you could easily prepare a Codicil that removes your brother's name and adds a new executor.

On the other hand, if you want to change your entire distribution and set up trusts, you should probably get a new Will done.

The test I've always used to determine whether a client needs a Codicil or a whole new Will is the clarity test. Simply put, I look at the potential for anything in the documents to become confusing or questionable. If a Codicil has any chance at all of messing up the estate plan, then I recommend a new Will.

I've seen as many as six Codicils attached to one Will, which in my view is asking for trouble. Think about it. The Will is document A. Codicil B changes Will A. Codicil C changes Will A. Codicil D changes Codicil B. Codicil E changes Will A and Codicil D. The potential for mix-ups is tremendous.

I also recommend a whole new Will rather than a Codicil if the original Will is not particularly strong, or is lacking a full set of executor's powers.

So can you use a Codicil? As always, it depends on the situation.

UPDATE. THE USE OF CODICILS IS QUICKLY DISAPPEARING IN THIS DIGITAL AGE WHERE IT IS JUST AS FAST AND INEXPENSIVE TO CREATE A WHOLE NEW WILL AS IT IS TO MAKE A CODICIL. THEY MAY STILL BE USED SELECTIVELY, PARTICULARLY WHERE CAPACITY AT THE TIME OF THE CODICIL MIGHT ONE DAY BE QUESTIONED, BUT THEY ARE DEFINITELY BECOMING MORE RARE.

If I die without a Will, my wife gets everything. Doesn't she?

20, 562 views

Something I hear quite often from people is that they are not going to make a Will because they are married and they believe that everything they own will, because of the fact that they are married, go to their spouse when they pass away. Unfortunately, this is not necessarily the case.

Every province and territory in Canada has a law which says what happens to the property of someone who dies without a Will. In Alberta, it's the Intestate Succession Act. This law works together with other arrangements you've made, such as beneficiary designations (in insurance policies, RRSPs, pension plans etc.) and joint titles (such as on your home or cottage). This combination of laws will decide who gets what from your estate when you pass away without a Will.

When you pass away, if you are married and everything you own is either in joint names with your spouse or designates your spouse as the beneficiary, then yes, your spouse will get everything you own. If you have any assets that are in your own name, then those assets are governed by the Intestate Succession Act.

The Act says that if you pass away leaving a spouse and one child (legitimate or otherwise, a minor or adult) then your spouse gets the first $40,000 of your assets and the rest is split evenly between your spouse and your child. If you leave a spouse and more than one child, the spouse gets the first $40,000 and one third of the rest. The other two thirds are divided equally among the children.

Note that this distribution includes children of previous relationships as they are your biological children. It also includes adult children with whom you might not have a relationship at all.

UPDATE: ALBERTA NO LONGER HAS AN INTESTATE SUCCESSION ACT, AS IT WAS REPLACED BY THE WILLS ESTATES AND SUCCESSION ACT. HOWEVER, ALL PROVINCES IN CANADA HAVE SOME FORM OF INTESTATE LAW IN PLACE THAT SETS OUT WHO GETS WHAT WHEN SOMEONE DIES WITHOUT A WILL. THOUGH THE NUMBERS CHANGE FROM PLACE TO PLACE, THE PRINCIPLES ARE THE SAME EVERYWHERE.

If you still have, for example, a life insurance policy that names your first spouse or your parents, that policy will still be paid to your named beneficiaries. If you own a cottage with your brother as joint tenants, the cottage will go to your brother and your spouse will not inherit any share of the cottage.

People are often surprised, and not always in a good way, when they realize how intestacy laws would apply to them and their families. It is a huge mistake to assume that you know how the law would apply to you when you have never asked a lawyer. If you have a family, you should have a Will properly prepared by a lawyer.

Can I leave my child out of my Will?

5,398 views

When planning their Wills, parents usually put quite a bit of thought into what they want to leave to their children. Occasionally a parent doesn't want to leave anything to a particular child. There are plenty of good reasons for this. It could be because the parent and child are estranged. It could be because the parent gave the child quite a bit of financial help while the parent was alive. It could be because the parent really wants to leave it to someone else (either a person or a charity). Perhaps the parents have left an insurance policy or other property directly to that child.

Whether or not a parent would be successful in leaving a child out of the Will depends in large part on whether the child is either a minor, or an adult child who can't earn a living because of a handicap. Children who fall into those two categories are considered to be financial dependents of the parent and can't be left out of the Will without a significant risk that the Will would be contested.

UPDATE: NOTE THAT BRITISH COLUMBIA HAS WILLS VARIATION LAWS WHICH ALLOW ADULT CHILDREN TO CONTEST A PARENT'S WILL ON FAIRNESS GROUNDS. THE REST OF CANADA DOES NOT HAVE THAT LAW.

121

Because adult children who are not handicapped do not have an automatic right to contest the parent's Will to get a larger share, the parent does not legally have to leave the child anything. This is an area where real life isn't as simple as the legal rules. A parent who leaves a child out of a Will is going against the expectations of the child and likely of everyone else. A child who is left out of the Will generally feels punished and wonders what he or she did to upset Mom or Dad.

Plenty of people think it's the law that they must leave their estates to their children and that they must treat all children equally in their Wills, but it isn't. It is, however, a strong cultural tradition that children inherit from parents, so if the parent plans to do something else with the estate, he or she is working against a very strong tradition and an even stronger expectation.

Whenever a client of mine wants to do something in a Will which may not seem logical or obvious to other people, I include a clause that briefly explains the person's reasons for taking this route. For example, if a parent were to leave a child out of the Will, the Will would contain a sentence or two giving the facts that the parent won't be around to give in person. It could say that the parties are estranged, or that the child has already been supported by joint property given to him or her. The purpose of including a clause like this is to make it clear to anyone reading the Will that the testator had put thought into the decision, knew that he or she had a child who expected to inherit, and that he or she made a different choice anyway.

Sometimes Wills are attacked on the basis that the testator (in this case the parent) didn't "know what he or she was doing". Having a rational explanation included goes a long way towards refuting that kind of claim.

If you are thinking of leaving one or more of your children out of your Will, please talk to an estate-planning lawyer about this. If you want to do this because of an ongoing problem between you and your child, also talk to the lawyer about how you will be able to protect yourself financially if you should lose mental capacity.

Leaving an inheritance to the children of the first marriage

3,364 views

As people enter into second and subsequent marriages, they generally don't mix their assets with their new spouses the way they did with their first spouse. There are plenty of reasons for this, of course, but one major consideration is the fact that people often wish to ensure that one day their children will inherit something from them. Parents can feel quite strongly that they want their children of the first marriage to have the benefit of the estate both of their parents built up together.

It's a topic I am asked about frequently, so when this reader wrote to me with a question about it, I thought I'd share the question and my answer below:

> *"If someone remarries after death of a spouse, how does that person leave an inheritance to their natural children and not have everything go to their second wife? Is that done through the will?"*

Your will is very important for ensuring that the distribution you want is going to happen.

In your will you can specify assets that are going to go to your children. In a first marriage, a person's will often says that assets are all to be given to the spouse, and only on the death of both parents are the children to inherit. In a second marriage scenario, the will might be very different and set up a split of assets between the children and the spouse.

In some cases, these might be assets that will be needed for a while by your spouse before your children can have them. For example, you might want to make sure that your second spouse will be able to live in the family home should she outlive you, but you may want your kids to own that house one day. To do this, you could set up a trust that would pass the house on to your children once your new spouse has passed away.

There are other viable trusts too, such as family trusts that name your children and yourself as beneficiaries.

Just a warning here. Do not, under any circumstances, try to write a trust like this yourself. Believe me when I say there are dozens of rules about trusts that you don't know.

Now let's talk about the limitations of using your will to give assets to your children. Your will is not the only legal paper that comes into play after you pass away. Remember that your will doesn't change some of the other arrangements that you may already have in place. The two main areas that I refer to are jointly held property, and property with a designated beneficiary. Pre-nuptial agreements may also have an effect on your will.

As an example, if you and your second wife own your home jointly with a right of survivorship, you can't leave it to your children (or anyone else for that matter) in your will. Even if you put it into your will, it won't do anything. In a case like this, your second wife will own the property after you pass away because she is a joint owner.

Assets with a named beneficiary also pass outside of your estate and therefore are not governed by your will. As an aside, it IS possible to use your will to change a beneficiary designation but that is not the best way to do so. Assets like RRSPs and life insurance policies have beneficiaries that you name at the time you set up your RRSP or buy your policy. This named beneficiary gets the proceeds of the plan or the policy on your death. If you have named your new spouse as the beneficiary of a plan or policy, your will doesn't affect those assets.

Keep in mind though, that you can name your children as beneficiaries of insurance policies too.

The final downside to using your will to leave assets to your children is that your spouse may decide to challenge your will to try to obtain a larger share of the estate. A lawyer can draft your will and set up your assets in a way that will help reduce the odds of that kind of challenge.

So to pull this all together, a person who wants to leave assets to his children from his first marriage should make a list of all of his assets, including his home, cottage, business, bank accounts, investments, pension, insurance policies, vehicles, and anything else he might own. This list would include things he only owns part of, for example his share of a cabin he owns with his siblings. Then he should list how each asset is held. By that I mean he should indicate whether the asset is owned by him alone, or whether he owns it together with another person. For assets that carry a beneficiary designation, he should write down who that is.

Using this list, he can now get a clear picture of what assets will be available for him to leave to his children, and which would be covered by his will. It makes a lot of sense to take that list to an estate planning lawyer for a brain-storming session, as there are usually taxes or other surprises that people don't see coming.

Another option is to give your children assets while you're alive, assuming that there are assets you can part with, without reducing your ability to look after your own needs as you age. For example, you could pass on the family business to the children, or give sums of money. I'm not suggesting putting your kids' names on your accounts or your house, as that is one of the worst ideas of all time, but that you give them some of your assets if you want to, and can afford to.

While a will can be an excellent tool for ensuring that the children of your first marriage receive an inheritance, your will is only part of the solution. It's a tricky and important question, so please sit down with a lawyer and talk it all through.

Why use a spousal trust in estate planning?
3,586 views

A trust exists whenever one person (the trustee) is holding money or property on behalf of another person (the beneficiary). A spousal trust generally means that some or all of an estate is being held in trust for the use of the spouse of the deceased person. A spousal trust is usually for the entire lifetime of a spouse, but the length of the trust may vary depending on what the trust is intended to achieve.

When property or funds are held in a trust, the beneficiary doesn't own the assets, but only has use of them. For example, if there is a house in the trust, the beneficiary can live in the house but cannot sell it. When money is held in trust, the beneficiary usually receives the amount that is described in the trust, but not the full capital of the fund. Trusts are very flexible instruments, and many of the details can be tailored to the situation at hand.

There are a number of reasons that spousal trusts are used in estate planning.

Spousal trusts are often used in blended family situations where the individual making a will wants to pass his or her estate to their children of a previous marriage. A woman in a second marriage might leave her home in a trust for her spouse so that he can continue to reside there if he outlives her, but he can't sell the property. The terms of the trust would say that when the spouse passes away or can no longer live in the house, it will become the property of the woman's children.

I've also seen a spousal trust used where the will was made fairly late in the testator's life, at a time when the spouse

128

was already beginning to lose capacity. The testator was worried that someone might take financial advantage of the surviving spouse if she were left to manage a large sum of money. As a result, the funds were put into a trust instead in order to protect the spouse.

Spousal trusts can also be used to protect some assets from capital gains tax. For example, if a husband and wife own shares in their privately-owned company, and the wife passes away, her shares are subject to capital gains tax. However, the shares can be rolled over to a spousal trust so that taxes aren't payable and the business can carry on without a financial hit.

And along the tax-savings line, a spousal trust can be used where the surviving spouse already has significant income and giving him or her the estate would result in extra tax being levied. A trust is a separate tax payer and can pay tax each year on the income earned on its assets. In a case like this, you might even see the spouse named as the trustee or one of the trustees for his or her own trust.

If you are considering setting up a spousal trust in your own will, make sure you talk out the pros and cons of the idea with your estate planning lawyer. If you are considering using a trust for either of the tax reasons mentioned here, talk to your accountant before you go ahead. One sentence seen here on mu blog is sufficient to point out the possibility, but you need one-on-one advice before you take any steps.

ᴅoes every Will have to be probated?

176,865 views

This is one of those questions that I am asked over and over again, so I thought I'd mention it here. The short answer to the question is "no", but that doesn't tell the whole story.

Probate is not needed to transfer certain kinds of assets. Specifically, you do not need probate to transfer property that is held in joint names. This is because joint ownership carries with it a right of survivorship of the other owner(s). For example, if a husband and wife own their home jointly and the wife passes away, the husband owns the house by right of survivorship and doesn't need probate to put the title in his name alone. Take note that this rule does not necessarily apply to assets that were jointly owned by the deceased and his or her children.

You also do not need probate to transfer assets that have a named beneficiary. These assets include RRSPs, RRIFs, life insurance policies, pensions and some other assets. When the owner of the asset passes away, you only need to provide a Death Certificate and some information in order to transfer that asset to the person who is named.

 Because of these rules, it's quite possible, and in fact is the norm, that a husband and wife can set up their financial affairs using joint property and beneficiary designations so that when one of them dies, the other one does not need to go through probate.

For anyone who is not in that situation, and whose assets are not all going to pass to someone automatically due to joint tenancy or beneficiary designation, the question of whether probate is needed is going to depend at least partly on the type of asset they own.

If you own real estate in your own name alone, or if you own it as a tenant-in-common, your executor will need a Grant of Probate to transfer or sell your property.

If you have assets that will form part of your estate after you die, such as life insurance policies and RRSPs that name your estate as beneficiary, your Executor will need to get probate. This also applies to any assets held in your name alone, such as a bank account, investment, or expensive personal items (e.g. art collection).

If you have a significant amount of money in your estate, your Executor will need probate before he or she can gain access to it.

There are other, less common, reasons why executors must go through probate. For example, the executor might have to finish litigating a lawsuit on behalf of the deceased. There could be a dependent who wants to make a claim against the estate. There could be some question about whether the Will itself is valid or some of its terms might need to be clarified.

It's sometimes hard to tell right at the beginning of an estate whether or not you need to go through the probate process. Sometimes the only way to know for sure is to take the Will to an experienced lawyer, together with information about the deceased person and his or her assets, and ask for an opinion.

The "Avoiding Probate at all Costs" Issue

8,531 views

One of the questions that I am asked on a regular basis is how to avoid probate. The concept of avoiding probate is raised in articles and blogs all over Canada and it is usually promoted as something we should all try to do. The reason given for avoiding probate is that probate fees can be high. The usual advice is to put property into joint names (usually with your children) to circumvent the probate process.

This is where people need to stop and consider the facts. In Alberta, we have the lowest probate court fees in the country. The highest your probate fee can be is $400, no matter how many millions of dollars are in your estate. If you are reading articles that say that probate fees will run into the tens of thousands of dollars, the article is probably written in Ontario or British Columbia, where probate fees are a percentage of the estate and are very high

Having established that the number you are working to avoid is $400, you need to think about what you are risking by putting your property into joint names with your children. While having property in joint names between husband and wife is usually a good idea, I almost never advise putting it in joint names with your children.

Consider the case where Mr. and Mrs. Smith put their home in joint names with their son, Joe. They do this only to avoid probate at some future time. A few years later, Joe gets divorced from his wife. Legally, he is just as much an owner of the Smiths' home as they are. Now they risk losing their home and tens of thousands of dollars in equity because they tried to avoid paying a $400 court fee.

Unfortunately, quite a few people have already taken this step without legal advice. I rarely give a presentation without someone approaching me afterward to say they have already put their home in joint names with their children and asking whether it was a good idea. I do not mean to say there is never a good reason for putting assets in joint names with children, but in my opinion, if it is done solely to avoid probate, it may not be the best solution when balanced against the risk.

UPDATE: BE SURE TO READ POSTS IN THIS BOOK DEALING WITH JOINT PROPERTY AND ADDING CHILDREN'S NAMES TO PROPERTY TO GET A FULL PICTURE OF THE "AVOIDING PROBATE" ISSUE.

Before putting your assets - either real estate or investments - into joint names with your children, find out the facts and the risks by talking it over with an experienced estate planning lawyer. The whole idea behind estate planning is to set things up so that they run smoothly and give you peace of mind, and putting joint names on property may do just the opposite.

What does probate REALLY cost?
100,119 views

With all this talk about probate and avoiding probate, it's important to have the facts. I'm often asked what probate costs. I know the people who ask me that would love a really short answer, such as "it costs $100", but realistically that short answer doesn't exist. What probate will cost depends on where in Canada you live, and what assets are in the estate.

When we talk about the cost of probate, strictly speaking the answer should be about what the court will charge you to process the probate application. To me, though that answer is essential, it's not the whole picture. The other half of the picture is the fee charged by the lawyer. In this post I'll look at both.

First of all, court fees (otherwise known as probate fees). If you apply for probate, there is no way to avoid paying a fee, even if you don't use a lawyer. Each province and territory is different and a chart of the court probate fees by province is shown at the end of this post. There is no fee or a very low fee for smaller estates. The areas of Canada that have a **maximum** fee are Alberta ($400) and Quebec ($65). In every other province and territory, the fee continues to increase as the size of the estate increases and there is no upper limit. This is one of the main reasons individuals like to do estate planning - they'd rather arrange things so that the money ends up with their families and not the "taxman".

Secondly, lawyer's fees. Again, they change from one place to another. It's not unusual for a lawyer to charge a percentage of the estate (up to 2%, but less for larger estates). However, it's more common that a lawyer will charge by the hour. This is because it's not always possible at the beginning of a matter to determine how long it's going to take to do the job. "Getting probate" is a complicated process if the deceased owned property that needs to be appraised, or had accounts in several banks and brokerages, or owned assets overseas.

Alberta	$25 for estates under $10,000 $100 for estates between $10,000 and $24,999 $200 for estates between $25,000 and $124,999 $300 for estates between $125,000 and $249,999 $400 for estates of $250,000 or more
British Columbia	$0 for estates under $10,000 $208 for estates between $10,001 and $25,000 $6 for every $1,000 (or part of $1,000) by which the value of the estate exceeds $25,000 but is not more than $50,000 Plus $14 for every $1,000 (or part of $1,000) by which the value of the estate exceeds $50,000
Manitoba	$50 for the first $10,000 $6 for every $1,000 by which the value of the estate exceeds $10,000
New Brunswick	$5 for each $1,000
Newfoundland and Labrador	$85 for the first $10,000 $5 for every $1,000 by which the value of the estate exceeds $10,000 Plus $50 for the probate Order
Northwest	$25 for estates under $10,000

Territories	$100 for estates between $10,000 and $25,000 $200 for estates between $25,000 and $125,000 $300 for estates between $125,000 and $250,000 $400 for estates worth $250,000 or more
Nova Scotia	$70 for estates under $10,000 $176 for estates between $10,000 and $25,000 $293 for estates between $25,000 and $50,000 $820 for estates between $50,000 and $100,000 Plus $13.85 for each $1,000 (or part of $1,000) by which the value of the estate exceeds $100,000
Nunavut	$25 for estates under $10,000 $100 for estates between $10,000 and $25,000 $200 for estates between $25,000 and $125,000 $300 for estates between $125,000 and $250,000 $400 for estates worth $250,000 or more
Ontario	$5 for each $1,000 for the first $50,000 Plus $15 for each $1,000 (or part of $1,000) by which the value of the estate exceeds $50,000
Prince Edward Island	$50 for estates up to 10,000 $400 for estates from $10,001 to $100,000 Plus $4 for each $1,000 (or part of

	$1,000) by which the value of the estate exceeds $100,000 Plus closing fee of 0.2%
Quebec	$0 for notarial wills $65 for non-notarial wills
Saskatchewan	$7 for every $1,000 (or part of $1,000) of estate value
Yukon	$0 for estates up to $25,000 $140 for estates that exceed $25,000

The mythical "will that doesn't need probate"
8,118 views

Earlier this week I spoke with a customer who told me that some years ago he had asked for, and paid his lawyer for, a "Will that doesn't need probate". He seemed annoyed when I told him that based on the assets he currently owned, his Will would have to be probated if he should pass away.

There is no such thing as a "Will that doesn't need probating" – at least in the sense of knowing at the time it's written that it will never need to go to probate - because the Will itself is not the only determinant of whether probate is necessary. Whether or not you need to probate someone's Will often depends on what kind of assets they own, and how those assets are held (e.g. jointly owned, owned solely but with a designated beneficiary, etc.). If you own certain assets, your Will must be probated, or if you don't have a Will, someone must be appointed as an administrator.

The customer I was dealing with owned a mineral title. On talking with me in more detail, he remembered that the lawyer had said if he didn't want his Will to be probated, he had to change or get rid of his mineral title. The customer hadn't done that.

An estate plan is a jigsaw puzzle, and the pieces are the Will, the assets, the family, the beneficiary designations, the jointly owned property, the incapacity documents (Power of Attorney and health-care directive) and the taxes. All of the pieces have to work together.

When you ask an estate-planning lawyer for a "Will that doesn't need probate", what you are really asking is for a plan in which all of your assets are dealt with during your lifetime. This is achievable, as long as you're willing to own absolutely everything from your car to your business to your bank account in joint names with other people, or to name beneficiaries (where that is possible) other than your estate. This is generally only practical for married people and even then, not always. People do get divorced, after all.

You have to ask yourself why you'd live your life that way just to avoid probate. Particularly in those provinces where the probate fees are low, probate isn't expensive so it simply makes no sense to put your assets at risk this way. You may think that avoiding probate is simpler, but if you have to change the ownership of everything you own, and possibly lose some of those assets to other people, is that really easier?

So if you're thinking of asking your lawyer for a "Will that doesn't need probate", get the facts about probate first. Don't rely on anecdotes told by co-workers or friends about what they think happens on estates. If you're reading advice in magazines or blogs, check with a lawyer in your area to see whether it applies to you. Think about whether avoiding probate is actually worthwhile - and workable - for you.

What is "resealing" probate?

6,765 views

"Resealing" is the process of having the local provincial or territorial court confirm a Grant of Probate from another jurisdiction. Usually when a person passes away, the Grant of Probate that is obtained from the court is sufficient to deal with all of the assets the person owns. However, when there is real property (land, house, cottage, mineral rights, etc.) in another province or territory, or assets of any kind in Commonwealth countries, the Grant of Probate is not enough.

For example, a Grant of Probate from Alberta is not sufficient to transfer land in Ontario. The Alberta Grant of Probate would have to be resealed in Ontario.

I've had to obtain resealed Grants in England, Scotland and Isle of Jersey and in each case it was time-consuming but went smoothly enough. It's not something you would try to do without legal assistance.

The process is very similar to applying for the original Grant of Probate. It can't be exactly the same, because the original Will is not available, having already been submitted to the first court. The other major difference is that the first Grant of Probate would have included a detailed inventory of all kinds of assets and debts. The resealing application will only address the real property (and any related debts etc.) that is in the new jurisdiction. This means that the probate/resealing court fee is usually significantly smaller than the original application.

Canadian courts will reseal Grants of Probate from all Canadian provinces and territories, as well as all

Commonwealth countries. Commonwealth countries will reseal a Grant of Probate from Canada.

What is an estate freeze?

4,194 views

An estate freeze is a way of transferring ownership of a privately held corporation, often between family members, by reorganizing the company. The freeze has two purposes. One is to transfer ownership of the company from one owner to another. The second is to limit the capital gains tax for the business owner who is transferring his or her shares to someone else. Both of these things happen at the same time.

Before the freeze, the business owner usually holds common shares of his or her business. Common shares give the share owner a stake in the profits and direction of a company. Usually a common share does not give the owner a right to receive a dividend but instead represents a share of the overall value of the company itself. As the value of the corporation grows, the value of the common share also grows. Another important feature of a common share is that it almost always gives its owner a vote in the running of the corporation.

On the day agreed on for the estate freeze, the business owner exchanges those common shares for preferred shares that have a fixed monetary value. At this point, the old owner is owed a specified sum of money for the ownership of the business. That sum of money is represented by the new preferred shares. The sum of money might also be secured by putting a promissory note into place in addition to the preferred shares.

The new preferred shares can either be shares of the operating business itself or can be shares of a holding company. They will never increase in value even if the common shares increase in value. The new preferred shares can be voting shares or non-voting shares, depending on what the business owner and the successor have agreed, although it would be more usual for the old owner to receive non-voting shares.

The outgoing business owner is liable for capital gains tax on the increase in value of the business from the day he acquired it to the day of the freeze. The new owner is liable for the tax from the day of the freeze onward.

Business owners might discuss the possibility of an estate freeze with their estate planning lawyers, corporate lawyers and accountants. For a detailed background discussion of estate freezes, see my book "Succession Planning Kit for Canadian Business."

Are "in trust for" bank accounts really trusts?

3,257 views

Many parents and grandparents set up accounts at a bank to save money for their child or grandchild. They set up the accounts as being "in trust for" (or, ITF) the child or grandchild. These accounts are popular, largely because the set-up is so simple. The idea is that the parent or grandparent puts money in the account, which grows until the child or grandchild reaches the age of majority and receives the funds.

But are these accounts really trusts? And if they are, what does that mean for the parent or grandparent who contributes the money? And what does it mean for the child?

Yes, these accounts are trusts. They may not seem like it, given that there is no deed, will or other document drawn up by a lawyer. Because of this, ITF accounts are known as informal trusts, but they are still trusts.

The basic nature of a trust is that money is held by a trustee (in this case the parent or grandparent) on behalf of a beneficiary (in this case a child or grandchild). Because it's a trust, the money can only be used for the beneficiary. The trustee has a legal obligation to do this. The trust is irrevocable, meaning that the contributing parent or grandparent can't change his or her mind after the account is set up and take the money back out for their own use.

If the child named as the beneficiary reaches the age of majority, he or she will receive the full amount of the funds and any interest earned on the funds. If the child doesn't reach the age of majority, the funds in the ITF account do NOT automatically go back to the parent or grandparent.

144

The funds fall into the child's estate. Odds are good that the child won't have a will, since he or she is under the age of majority. In that case, the funds would be distributed according to the law of intestacy in the province where the child or grandchild lives.

As an example, Ian's grandmother sets up an ITF account for Ian to receive when he turns 18 years old. Unfortunately Ian is killed in an accident when he is 16 years old. He doesn't have a will. The ITF account becomes part of Ian's estate, which according to the law of intestacy goes to his parents. The parents receive the ITF funds.

Make sure you mention any ITF accounts you've set up for your children or grandchildren when you meet with your estate-planning lawyer.

Does the share of a deceased beneficiary go to her husband?

3,109 views

What happens if a beneficiary named in a will dies before the testator of the will? This question was recently asked of me by a reader. Here's the question:

> *"My father wrote a will long time ago and named my mom, my brother, my 2 sisters and I as the beneficiaries but unfortunately, one of my sisters died 10 years ago. Will her husband and her only son take her part and become beneficiaries? Her husband has got married right after my sister's death. Should my father delete my sister's name from the will if he does not want to leave money to her husband?"*

There are two major considerations to keep in mind when looking at a situation like this. One is what the will says, and the other is what happens if the will doesn't address it.

Your father should take out his will and check what it says. The exact wording of a will always matters (which is why I don't really like people making their own wills). For example, if the will says your father leaves the estate to the four children "or the survivor of them", then your sister's share would be divided among the surviving three children. However, most people don't set their wills up that way unless their children are pretty young. You did say the will was made a long time ago so it's possible.

As another example, if your father's will says that a deceased child's share is to be divided per stirpes, the share would pass down to your sister's son.

Normally a will says that the share of a deceased child would be given to that child's children, simply because this is what most people choose. Also, in most places, this is what would happen under intestacy law if there were no will in place or the will didn't mention it.

Your sister's husband is not going to be entitled to your sister's share unless the will specifically says that he is. In my experience, most people choose to pass inheritances down through the family bloodlines and it's pretty rare that they leave a child's share to the child's spouse. Also, if the will doesn't mention what happens, there is no law that says he must get her share. Whether or not he re-married is not relevant.

When you take both of these considerations together, it seems unlikely that your sister's husband is going to get her share, but without seeing the will itself obviously I can't know for sure. This is important stuff for your father, for your siblings and for your sister's son. It's better to clear up questions now while your father is able to address them than to wait until it's too late.

A problem with some older wills is that the la9nguage can be archaic and hard to understand. This could be an impediment for your father as he reviews the document on his own. If your father finds that he really can't tell what the heck the will means on this question, he should make an appointment with a wills and estates lawyer to review his will. Ideally, I would like to see your father sit down with an experienced lawyer to explain what he wants to do with his estate and have the chance to ask whether his current will meets his needs. He would achieve peace of mind by knowing that the proper document is in place.

Keep in mind that wills laws and tax rules change over time and older wills should be reviewed from time to time to make sure they are still current. This will go a long way to ensuring that there will be no problems administering your father's estate when that time comes.

It also occurs to me that if he made his will such a long time ago, he might not have made a Power of Attorney or a health care directive. Maybe this is the time to re-visit all of this. It's great that all of you are discussing these issues as a family and that you seem prepared to help your parents get everything into place. I strongly urge your father to see an experienced lawyer and talk all of this through.

How can I make sure that my daughter-in-law gets none of my son's inheritance?

2,572 views

Recently I had a conversation with a client I'll call Doris, who told me that she is not particularly fond of her daughter-in-law. Doris's reason for consulting me was to find out how she can leave her estate to her son without her daughter-in-law getting any of it. It might surprise you just how many parents bring up this topic. I encourage my clients to speak openly about any and all concerns that might relate to their estates, and this is certainly one that is mentioned frequently. Because of its frequency, I thought other readers might be interested in hearing about the topic.

The first thing for anyone in Doris's situation to understand is that if you leave your estate outright to your son or daughter, there is absolutely nothing you can say in your will to prevent him or her from sharing that inheritance with his or her spouse. Also, there is nothing you can say or do to prevent some or all of that inheritance from going to the spouse when your son or daughter dies, or they get divorced. There is nothing you can say or do to prevent that surviving spouse from marrying someone else and leaving the money to his or her new spouse and not to your grandchildren. Once you give money away, you can't control what someone else does with that gift.

That probably isn't what you want. It certainly wasn't what Doris wanted. I thought she might faint when I mentioned her daughter-in-law possibly marrying someone else and the inheritance going to that new family.

So, let's look at a solution.

In Canada, money that is inherited is generally exempt from division if a husband and wife should get divorced. In some provinces, the legislation allows for a clause to be put into a will confirming that any inheritance under the will is not intended to become family property. However, there are two problems with this as a solution to Doris's situation.

The first is that if Doris leaves money to her son and he uses the funds to buy something that is put into joint names, such as a home, the funds are in jeopardy. At best, there would be endless legal wrangling and calculations to figure out whether some portion of the home should be bought out by the daughter-in-law, and at worst the funds would simply be gone. Similarly, the son might spend the money on gifts for his wife such as expensive jewelry, or on vacations for both of them.

The second problem is that this only covers divorce. It doesn't do anything at all in the event that Doris's son dies and leaves his estate to his wife.

The answer to this situation is simply a trust. The inheritance for Doris's son should be placed in a trust when Doris passes away. Nothing needs to be done with the money right now; the trust doesn't get set up until Doris has died and her will comes into force.

When Doris's will is written, she will have the opportunity to decide when and why money will be parceled out by the trustee to Doris's son. It could be set up so that her son would receive a set amount of money each month or year. However, Doris indicated that she would like to restrict her son's access to funds, and limit him to receiving funds only for emergencies, or for education expenses for Doris' grandchildren. This is easily written into a will; trusts are very flexible.

Using a trust, Doris can ensure that:

- if her son and daughter-in-law should get divorced, her daughter-in-law won't get half of the funds.

- if her son passes away, the funds in trust won't go to his wife. Doris wants the trust set up so that on her son's death, any funds remaining in trust will go to her grandchildren.

- the daughter-in-law will not become trustee of the money for the children. Doris is naming a trust company to manage the trust for her son, and if necessary the grandchildren.

There are always drawbacks to any solution. In this case, the drawbacks may be small compared to what is being accomplished, but it's important for anyone in Doris's situation to know what he or she is getting into. The drawbacks to using a trust to hold the inheritance are:

- many lawyers charge more to draft wills that have trusts in them.

- there is a cost associated with paying a trustee to manage the trust, as someone has to manage the money, prepare the tax returns, and send out the payments to the son.

- most importantly, Doris's son will never receive a large sum of money, and will never have the opportunity to use his inheritance to make a large purchase such as a cabin.

Taking all of these factors into consideration, a trust is the best tool available for this tricky family situation.

Beneficiaries' rights

Accurate, reliable information for beneficiaries seems to be among the hardest information to find. While there are plenty of books and articles available to assist executors to do their job, and a plethora of books for those planning their wills, there is little available for beneficiaries who are already in the midst of a worrisome estate.

I receive a steady stream of emails and questions from beneficiaries that boil down to "can the executor do that?" In some cases, they are pretty sure that the executor has gone off the rails and is stealing, or perhaps fudging the books to hide losses. In many other cases, they don't necessarily believe the executor is doing anything wrong, but the lack of information from the executor has them baffled and sometimes angry.

When I address questions from beneficiaries, I try to make a clear division between what the executor may be doing wrong and what the executor appears to be doing right. In plenty of cases, the executor isn't actually wrong at all; it is the beneficiaries' unfamiliarity with the legal system and the rules of estates that is causing them to be suspicious. Those are very satisfying queries to answer because I feel that the beneficiaries are well-served by finding out that things really are alright after all, and there is no need for panic.

I often advise beneficiaries to start by confirming what they believe to be the facts. It's very easy for families to get together to discuss an estate, and in so doing to pump up each other's suspicions by contributing inaccurate information. It's always worth it to spend a few dollars on a title search or court search to confirm what someone has said, and to ask for information in writing. This is also necessary if the beneficiaries eventually decide they must resort to the courts to resolve an issue.

In general, I find beneficiaries quite willing to take an executor to court. I expect there is an element of wanting to hit back at someone who has caused them extreme stress and conflict. However, I try to make it clear to beneficiaries and executors alike that going to court should be a last resort, due to the costs, time commitment, and most of all, the sheer ugliness of fighting it out with family members. The more time I spend in the legal system, the more I like the idea of mediation of estate issues.

When I inherit, how do I keep that money out of the hands of my spouse?
13,368 views

For the purposes of this discussion, let's assume that there was nothing in your parent's Will that either requires you to share your inheritance with your spouse, nor specifically prevents that from happening. In other words, this discussion is about YOUR actions and what effects they will have on money you inherit from your parents.

If you share your inheritance with your spouse, for example by using your inheritance to pay down a mortgage on a home that you and your spouse both own, then you cannot later decide to take it back. You've already turned your inheritance into joint property and given your spouse a gift of the money. Should you and your spouse later become divorced, the accounting and legal arguments involved in sorting out who owns what part of the home will become expensive and time-consuming.

Keeping a family inheritance separate sometimes becomes very important to individuals who are in second marriages. The individual's goal is often to ensure that the money inherited from his or her parents is passed on to his or her children. They feel that this is more in line with what the parents wanted, rather than have the money passed down through a son-in-law or daughter-in-law to step-grandchildren.

It is possible to keep the money separate. The person who inherits should open a separate account in his or her name only, and put the inheritance in there. Interest earned can accumulate in the account. Nothing else should be added. This way it remains easy to trace the origin of the money and it's clear that no joint money was ever added to it.

This matters if there is a divorce, because in most jurisdictions in Canada, money that was inherited by one of the people divorcing is exempt from being divided with the spouse. As described above, if you don't make sure that it's clearly inherited money and nothing else in the account, that account could be attacked and you could lose some of it.

When you make your Will, you can specifically leave that account to your children. I have always added a few words to my clients' Wills to identify the account as being one that was inherited from a parent. An alternative, of course, is to give some or all of your family inheritance to your children while you are alive, either by a direct transfer or by buying assets in joint names with them.

Can a person in bankruptcy inherit from an estate?

9,959 views

Here at Scotia Trust, one of our main tasks is to administer the estates of deceased persons who named us as their executor. As you can imagine with all of the estates that cross our desks, we see pretty much every situation sooner or later. Right now my colleagues are working on an estate in which one of the beneficiaries has declared bankruptcy, and has not yet been discharged.

UPDATE: AT THE TIME THIS POST APPEARED ON MY BLOG, I WORKED AS A WILLS AND ESTATES PLANNER FOR SCOTIA TRUST. I WORKED THERE FROM 2007 TO 2014.

A discharge of bankruptcy is an order of the court that says that the bankrupt person has fulfilled his or her obligations under the bankruptcy proceedings. Either all debts have been paid, or more likely, the property that was available for paying debts was divided up among creditors so that they were paid in part. While a person is undergoing the process and the court has not yet discharged him or her, any surplus income not needed for essentials is paid to the trustee in bankruptcy to be divided among the creditors.

If the person who is in bankruptcy is the beneficiary of an estate of someone who passed away, the bankrupt person's entire share of the estate will go to the trustee in bankruptcy. The trustee will use as much of the inheritance as is needed to pay all of the debts, even if this means the whole inheritance. If the trustee doesn't need all of the inheritance to pay the debts, then the surplus amount will be paid to the bankrupt person.

The bankrupt person can't legally waive his inheritance (i.e. decide he doesn't want it), and he can't assign it to someone else (i.e. say that he wants his inheritance paid to his wife or children or friends etc.). The trustee in bankruptcy has complete control over the bankrupt person's incoming money. The executor of the estate has no choice but to send the inheritance cheque to the trustee in bankruptcy.

If the bankrupt person has been discharged by the court and later inherits money, he is free to receive it just like anyone else.

Am I entitled to see my deceased parent's will?

10,315 views

Questions about a parent's estate stay with us, don't they? This is particularly true if we don't get a chance to see the will for ourselves. This reader asks a question that many others also wonder about. Here's the question:

> *"I am son to a father that left us at an early age. He had very little to do with me over the years and only ever paid the small court required child support until I turned 18. He was remarried and never had more kids that I am aware of. He passed away suddenly while I was in my 20s and I received no information or contact regarding his will. As a son would I not be entitled to see his will and if his death happened say 20 years ago and his wife is still alive today, could I do anything?"*

This question contains one of the most common misconceptions about wills out there. That a son or daughter is automatically entitled to see a deceased parent's will is assumed by many people. The assumption is wrong. There is no such entitlement.

Many people find this rule to be counter-intuitive. It makes sense to some people that a child should be entitled to see a parent's will. However, it simply isn't the case. You are not entitled to see a deceased person's will unless you are either the executor of the will or a residuary beneficiary of the will. Normally an executor would only contact those who were to inherit under the will.

A will is a private, personal document. As such, nobody is allowed to see it that has no legal reason to see it. Wanting to see it doesn't count. In my view, this is one more reason why people need to be super careful about who they appoint as executor, as we all know there are some executors out there who take advantage of privacy rules to deprive legitimate beneficiaries of their inheritance.

My guess would be that your father left his estate to his second wife and also made her the executor. If you (and any siblings) were over the age of 18 at the time and were not handicapped, you would not have been legal dependents and therefore he would not legally have to leave anything to you.

Your question about "doing anything" is a bit open-ended. If you are asking whether you could ask to see the will, yes you could, but you have no legal right to insist upon it. If you are asking whether you could get anything from the estate, I believe your chances are slim to none. In the absence of legal dependence on your father, what would be the basis for a challenge? And just as importantly, what would be left of the estate to collect on?

Can a beneficiary turn down an inheritance?

4,311 views

Recently I was asked this question at a seminar. Another audience member turned to the person asking the question and said, "Why would you want to turn it down?" I think that is the reaction of most people, but there are certainly cases where a beneficiary would rather not receive the inheritance.

I was involved in a case where a woman died without making a Will. She had a husband and three adult children. Most of the assets of the marriage, including the family home, were in her name. Under the laws of intestacy (i.e. dying without a Will), her estate was going to be divided between her husband and her children. This would leave the husband in very reduced financial circumstances. The children believed that the estate should have gone to their father and did not want to inherit their shares. They all turned down their inheritance in favour of their father.

It's unusual, but it happens.

Inheritances in Canada are not taxable, so accepting an inheritance won't cause you tax problems, even if you're already in a high tax bracket. However, accepting certain property might affect your finances. It could mean that you now to have to pay for maintenance and property tax on real estate, or pay insurance on valuable items.

It's also possible that a beneficiary might refuse an inheritance on purely emotional grounds. Dealing with the aftermath of the death of a loved one brings out strong emotions of every description.

If a beneficiary does not want to accept an inheritance, he or she can turn it down. It is a gift, not an obligation. It's referred to as waiving an inheritance.

To bring this about, the beneficiary would have to give the waiver in writing. There is no prescribed form of waiver in our Surrogate Rules of Court. In the cases that I've been involved in, I drafted a waiver form for the beneficiary to sign in front of a witness because I wanted the waiver to be clear and complete. I also wanted to make sure that beneficiaries were not being pressured by anyone to give up their inheritances.

The waiver form doesn't go to the court (unless there's some kind of dispute). The waiver is kept by the lawyer who acts for the estate/executor. Normally when someone waives a gift, the gift falls back into the residue of the estate and will then be paid or given to someone else in according to the Will, or according to the laws of intestacy. That is all arranged and fully documented by the estate lawyer before any money is paid out.

If my parents lend me money, do I have to repay it after they die?

5,107 views

Plenty of parents help out their children by lending money. Often it is for the down payment on a home, renovations or other major purchases. The amounts can be quite large. Sometimes the arrangement is formalized in a document, but most of the time it is not written down.

When the parent who has made a loan passes away, there is a question about whether or not the parent intended for the loan to be repaid. Often the child understands (or hopes, perhaps) that the money was a gift and the parent intended to forgive the loan all along.

But what happens if the parent makes a Will in which he or states that all of the children are to inherit equal shares? Does this mean that one child has received more than his or her share? And what if the parent died without making a Will at all? How should the loan be dealt with?

Let's look first at what happens if there is a Will. A parent can state in the Will whether or not he or she wants the loan to be forgiven. If the parent says in the Will that the children are to get equal shares of the estate but loans are to be forgiven, then the equal shares are calculated as if that loan had never been made.

If the parent says in the Will that the loan is not to be forgiven, then the child who received the money will receive less from the estate. It is rare that it actually involves the child repaying the loan. Unless the loan was larger than the share the child will inherit under the estate, it's simply a matter of subtracting the loan amount from the share. For example, if Sam was supposed to inherit $50,000 but had received a loan of $10,000 from his mother, and the mother's Will said the loan is not to be forgiven, then Sam will inherit only $40,000. This process is called set-off.

If a parent leaves a Will but doesn't say anything about loans to children, the executor must follow the general duty of collecting all debts owed to the deceased and his or her estate. This includes loans to children, so the child would have to repay it (or there would be set-off). This can be a real mess at times, for a couple of reasons. One is that if there is no documentation, the executor will have to prove the allegation that there was in fact money changing hands. This causes delays and usually friction between people as well. Another is determining the amount first loaned, and any amount repaid. The executor can't always count on co-operation from the child, for obvious reasons.

Now let's look at what happens if there is no Will and the parent has made a loan to a child. The Intestate Succession Act specifically states that in this case, any money given to a child is deemed by law to be a loan and not a gift. This would mean repayment or set-off. The same problems exist for establishing the amounts.

If you are a parent who has made a loan to one or more of your children, check your Will to see whether you've addressed the issue of repayment of loans. If not, do your children and your executor a big favour and deal with it so that nobody has to guess or litigate to figure out what you intended.

Why do residuary beneficiaries sign a release?

13,682 views

When the executor of an estate has finished cashing in assets and paying bills, has filed the tax returns and is ready to pay the beneficiaries, he or she will send the residuary beneficiaries a set of financial statements. Along with the statements will be a Release. If the executor is doing things properly, no residuary beneficiaries get their money until all of them have signed and returned the Release to the executor.

So what is the legal effect of that Release? What is the beneficiary really doing by signing it?

The financial statements that come with the Release are intended to give a full, accurate picture of all of the financial transactions the executor has done on behalf of the estate. The beneficiary should be able to tell from the statements what happened with every asset of the estate (e.g. the deceased's home was sold for $x and the money was put into the executor's account). The statements should show what was spent on the funeral, legal fees, accounting fees and other expenses. The beneficiary is entitled to ask for more detail if he or she believes that to be necessary.

By signing the Release, the beneficiary is approving of the financial statements and all that they contain. Releases will often refer to a time period, usually beginning on the date of death and continuing up until the day the Release was sent to the beneficiary. In those cases, the beneficiary is approving of everything the executor did during that time period. Sometimes in more complicated estates there will be more than one set of financials, perhaps with the second set a year or so after the first, but in most estates there is only one.

By signing the Release, the beneficiary is saying that he or she is satisfied with everything the executor has done. He or she is agreeing in writing that everything is fine. The beneficiary cannot later come back and find fault with the accounting, for example by saying that money is missing or that the house was sold for too little. The beneficiary is signing off on it and can't later change his or her mind.

This protects the executor from anyone coming back later and beginning a legal battle over something in the estate. Beneficiaries also benefit from it because the executor, who wants the Release to be signed, will usually provide a

UPDATE: AN EXECUTOR IS NOT ALLOWED TO REFUSE TO PAY A BENEFICIARY FOR NO REASON OTHER THAN TO FORCE THE BENEFICIARY TO SIGN A RELEASE. THE EXECUTOR SHOULD TRY TO GET A RELEASE, BUT IF THAT SIMPLY ISN'T POSSIBLE, THE EXECUTOR MAY CHOOSE TO PASS HIS ACCOUNTS THROUGH THE COURTS, THUS DISPENSING WITH THE NEED FOR THE BENEFICIARY'S SIGNATURE ON THE RELEASE.

thorough accounting that answers all of the beneficiaries' questions.

A beneficiary does have the right to have the accounting looked at by an accountant or a lawyer before signing the Release, though most do not. Every case is different and the beneficiary should take his or her time to read the accounting thoroughly before signing the Release and returning it to the executor.

I disagree with the executor's accounting - now what?

3,345 views

I hear a lot of questions from both executors and beneficiaries about the process of reviewing an executor's accounts and signing a Release. I recently received the following letter from a reader, which echoes what many others of you have asked:

> *"Can you tell me what happens if all heirs do not agree with the statement of accounts? Who looks at that and would the person(s) be contacted regarding why they do not agree with a statement of accounts? I disagreed with the statement of accounts over a year ago and nothing has happened with the will since. The executor is not co-operative."*

The beneficiaries of an estate are given the statement of accounts along with a Release. If all looks fine with the accounts, the beneficiaries sign the Releases and return them to the executor. Once all Releases have been received, the executor pays out the distribution that was outlined in the statement of accounts. The purpose of all of this is to get the beneficiaries to state that they approve of what the executor has done with the estate so far. This indemnifies the executor.

You asked who looks at the fact that a beneficiary doesn't agree with the accounting. This would be the executor. If the executor is using a lawyer to help with the estate, no doubt the executor would consult with the lawyer as to what to do next.

If the executor is trying to do the estate without the help of a lawyer and prepared the accounts without help from a lawyer or accountant, he or she may have no idea what to do now that a beneficiary has disagreed with the accounting. The next logical step from a legal point of view is for the executor to apply to the court to have the accounts passed by the court, but I would hope that before spending the time and money to do that, the executor would try to find out what the problem is, and rectify it.

Beneficiaries have the right to ask for more information on an accounting if something is unclear, or to ask about items that appear to have been omitted. And if the whole thing just seems out of whack, the beneficiary has the right to refuse to sign the Release.

UPDATE: THERE IS NO COURT OFFICIAL OR GOVERNMENT OFFICE WHOSE JOB IT IS TO REVIEW EXECUTORS' ACCOUNTING DOCUMENTS. THEY ARE ONLY REVIEWED BY COURT CLERKS IF THERE IS AN APPLICATION TO PASS ACCOUNTS, AND EVEN THEN, IT IS SIMPLY A CHECK TO SEE WHICH DOCUMENTS ARE BEING BROUGHT TO COURT. IT IS UP TO THE BENEFICIARIES TO POLICE THE ACCOUNTING.

Unfortunately, our system is based on the premise that an executor will want to take care of the estate properly and will make every effort to move the estate along as best he can. As it happens, plenty of executors don't really care if the estate drags on for years, as they aren't the ones waiting for an inheritance. Therefore, even if the executor is aware of the next steps, he or she may not wish to proceed without prodding.

You need to write a letter. If the accounting was sent to you by a lawyer, write to the lawyer, otherwise write directly to the executor. State your objections to the accounting, giving facts or figures if at all possible. Saying something like "I just don't like what you did" or "I think you're hiding something" isn't useful and won't bring anything to a conclusion. You should be able to specifically refer to an item or a figure, and state, for example, "Mom's house was listed for $450,000 but the accounting only shows $325,000 going into the bank. What happened to the rest?"

Your responsibility to the procedure is to police the executor's actions, but keep in mind that the executor is human and can make mistakes. Give him or her the chance to explain the numbers in the accounting. Realize that most of us have never provided an accounting for anything in our lives and perhaps aren't that good at it, so your detailed questions should allow the executor to understand what is required. Don't nit-pick for the sake of nit-picking, and try to stick to real issues.

Refer to the fact that the accounting was provided a year ago, and that you want the matter cleared up.

If you receive satisfactory answers to your questions, you should sign the Release and return it to the executor. As you've said that the executor isn't co-operative, I don't expect this to happen, but perhaps after a year he or she is more motivated to wrap it up. Don't sit and wait any longer; there is a common law concept of the executor's year that says an estate without legal complications should be wrapped up in a year, and obviously the executor has exceeded that.

If the executor simply won't move on it, you will likely have to hire a lawyer to help you resolve it or push it through court. Perhaps the other beneficiaries would pool their resources with you since everyone would stand to benefit.

Where are the "executor police" when you need them?

A question that Wills and Estates lawyers hear frequently is "what can I do about the executor?" The activities of the executor that cause concern can be anything from outright theft to simply doing nothing at all. And there is an unbelievable variety of things in between.

One of the most common examples of executor's behaviour that causes concern is distributing the deceased person's estate in a way that the executor thinks is fair, even though it's not what was directed in the Will. Obviously the role of executor is very poorly understood, because time and time again an executor will ignore the Will and pay out the estate according to his or her wishes, which is clearly not what he or she is supposed to do.

An example of this is an executor who divides the estate equally among him/herself and siblings, even though the parent's Will divided things a different way. I've asked executors over the years what the heck they thought they were doing by ignoring the Will, and the answer is always "but it's more fair this way", or some variation on "I didn't want to upset someone by leaving them less than the others".

This is not okay. The executor's job is to follow the Will, regardless of personal feelings. It's not the executor's money or the executor's decision. (As an aside, this is something that people need to consider when choosing an executor and one reason why family members don't necessarily make the best executors).

171

So who watches over these activities? Are there any executor police who keep an eye on executors? There is only one group of people who has the right to keep the executor on track with the Will. That group is made up of the residuary beneficiaries of an estate.

The residuary beneficiaries are the people who are sharing the bulk of the estate once bills have been paid, household and personal items have been divided, and specific gifts of cash have been made (such as to a charity).

When a residuary beneficiary has asked me for advice on what to do, and I've told them of their right to keep the executor on track, I sometimes get the response that the beneficiary doesn't want to make a fuss about who is getting what, because he or she doesn't want to look greedy. I understand that, and I agree with the general concept of not making waves that don't need to be made. However, a residuary beneficiary has not only the right to examine what the executor is doing, he or she also has an obligation to do so.

UPDATE: AN EXECUTOR WHO THINKS THAT THE WILL IS SO UNFAIR THAT HE CANNOT FOLLOW IT SHOULD RENOUNCE HIS ROLE, RATHER THAN TRY TO RE-WRITE THE WILL.

If the beneficiary knows that the executor, who has agreed to follow the Will by accepting the job as executor, is now

172

violating that agreement by ignoring the Will in full or in part, then the beneficiary should insist that the executor follow the Will. Who else is there to stand up for the deceased person if the executor is not doing so, other than the beneficiaries of the estate?

Some of the actions that can be taken against an executor who doesn't follow the instructions in the Will include removing the person as executor, causing the executor to lose his or her executor's fee, or even personal liability if the behaviour is egregious.

Can an executor be sued for secretiveness and delay?

5,235 views

I'd like to answer another excellent reader question today. The first thing I noticed about this question is that it starts with a complaint that the executor doesn't give any information. Executors reading this blog, take note at the number of problems that start when you hoard information! Just be transparent and a lot of these issues just don't ever arise.

Here is the reader's question:

> *"The executor does not give us any information about the estate of my mother, who died in 2004. He still does not want to settle the estate. He and his lawyer are saying there is an estate tax to be paid, which I believe is a capital gains tax as there are several piece of property involved. I was told that capital gains tax was paid in 2006. Now he is saying it is not. Can the beneficiaries sue the executor for lying for years?"*

The fact that capital gains tax was paid in 2006 but must be paid again doesn't necessarily mean the executor is lying. Keep in mind that capital gains tax is payable each time a piece of capital property such as real estate changes hands. Back in 2006, tax was paid on transfers of the property from 2004 to 2006. If property is now changing hands - say it's being transferred to a beneficiary or being sold to an independent buyer - then there likely is additional tax because of this transaction. After all, the properties have been sitting in the name of the estate for seven years and have probably gained in value during that time.

Having said that, in my view seven years is much too long for the wind-up of an estate. Obviously I don't know all of the facts, so there could be complications that I don't know about, such as farms or businesses on the lands in question. But any executor who takes seven years (so far) with an estate without at least giving regular reports to the residuary beneficiaries is taking a huge risk.

I'll never understand why executors are so darn secretive. Perhaps they think that it's better to just keep their mouths shut and not invite trouble by telling others what they're doing. Unfortunately this is almost always the wrong way to go about it and they just shoot themselves in the foot.

When an executor mishandles an estate (and I don't know for sure that this one has - I'm making a general statement here) he or she can be taken to courts by the beneficiaries. It isn't really suing the executor, in the familiar sense of suing for monetary damages. The usual outcomes are that the court will force an executor to pass accounts, or will remove an executor from the job, or will force the executor to lose his or her executor's fees, or all of the above. Executors are sometimes ordered to pay the estate out of their own pockets if their behaviour has been really over the top in terms of dishonesty or mismanagement.

This executor is fortunate that he hasn't already been taken to court. There may be nothing wrong at all with the estate, but if so, he hasn't let anyone know.

Help! The executor is stealing from the estate!

7,508 views

This post talks about what can happen to an executor who appears to be completely out of control. The question was sent in by a reader (thank you) about his or her particular circumstances but I believe a lot of readers out there will find the story to be a variation on their own situations:

> *"My grandmother died a year ago and my uncle was named executor in her will. He has not taken responsibility for any of the estate or assets. He was/is using her credit cards, vehicle, and anything else of hers that he left town with. My family does not know which step to take. We cannot confide in the lawyer that was being used due to the fact that he only deals with the executor. There isn't much money to hire another lawyer either. We do not know if there is anything we can do, or if there is even a case. My uncle often disappears and doesn't return phone calls. For all we know, there could be even more debt accumulated by him. Do you know what could happen to him on the part of fraud?"*

This question highlights the difference between criminal law and civil law. Although the vast majority of executors never get tangled up in criminal law, it does sometimes happen. Not as often as it should, in my view! It depends on the facts of the case. If the executor is using a deceased person's credit cards for his own personal gain and has stolen items from the estate, it sounds to me as if there is criminal activity taking place. Fraud and theft are still fraud and theft, though many executors mistakenly seem to think an estate is theirs to keep.

Fraudulent executors are pretty confident that nobody will notice what happens to estate assets, or that nobody would do anything even if they did notice. This is the crux of why so many executors steal from the very estates they are supposed to be protecting.

If you believe that fraud and/or theft have been committed, you don't have to hire a lawyer. You have to call the police. Having said that, it makes more sense if the call is made by a beneficiary of the estate rather than a family member who is not going to inherit from the estate. If the matter goes to court, the estate would be represented by the Crown Prosecutor.

When an executor misbehaves, it is most often dealt with using civil (non-criminal) law. That's because most problems with estates fall short of being outright theft. The problems tend to be things like executors who take too long, who don't look after assets and who won't tell the beneficiaries what's going on.

Proving your case can be difficult when you don't have access to documents or bank account statements. A criminal charge must be proven beyond a reasonable doubt. In a criminal case, the police or the prosecutor should be able to get whatever documents they need whether or not you personally have access to them. In a civil law case, you don't have to prove anything beyond a reasonable doubt; you have to prove your case only on the balance of probabilities (i.e. that it probably happened the way you say it did). If you can't get documents, the court may or may not order that some be given to you by the executor.

Using the civil law, a court can order, among many other things, that an executor must give a full accounting to beneficiaries or must meet certain deadlines. It can remove an executor from an estate, or can set how much of a fee (if any) the executor is going to receive.

On occasion, an executor decides to thumb his or her nose at a civil law court order, thinking that the worse that can happen is a loss of executor's fee. That's pretty foolish, as contempt of court may carry a jail sentence.

While you are certainly allowed to go to court without a lawyer for a civil law matter, it's very hard to do and you would be much better off if you had one.

Does no reading of the will mean the executor is hiding something?

3,563 views

I am asked this question so often that I wonder where the idea of a reading of the will comes from. Many people tell me that they expect a formal gathering of the entire extended family with the lawyer at the head of the table, reading the will word for word to the assembled crowd. I have only seen a reading of the will in that form in the movies.

A reading of the will in the sense of a family gathering is not something that is usually done. You should not assume that because there is no reading of the will that the executor is hiding something.
If the executor wishes, he or she can arrange for a meeting of the beneficiaries of the will and the lawyer. Sometimes executors want this because they feel that the lawyer will be better able to answer the beneficiaries' questions about particular assets, probate or timelines, particularly if the executor is feeling overwhelmed. It's completely optional though. And you'll notice that I didn't say a "meeting of the family". I said a "meeting of the beneficiaries". They may not be the same people.

As hard as it may be to hear, if you are not a beneficiary of a will, you are not entitled to have a copy of the will or see the will or be told what is in it. Many a pointless estate fight has been fought over this point, simply because an individual can't or won't accept that he's not entitled to know what's in a will. This is especially true when the deceased person is a parent.

179

Having said that, I'm well aware that not all executors are as trustworthy or as honest as the deceased had hoped they'd be. If I felt that the executor of an estate in my family was lying to me or stealing assets, you'd better believe that I'd push the point about seeing the will. I'd be prepared to accept the estate lawyer's written assurance that I'm not named in the will. (And for those of you who are quite sure that a lawyer would lie in these circumstances, ask yourself why on earth a lawyer would be prepared to be disbarred over your mom or dad's estate).

If you're an executor wondering whether you should hold a reading of the will, consider it as one more tool in your executor's toolkit, and use it if you think it will help matters along.

UPDATE: SINCE WRITING THIS POST, I HAVE HAD MORE EXPERIENCE WITH FORMAL READINGS OF WILLS. I FIND THEM EXTREMELY HELPFUL BOTH TO THE EXECUTOR AND TO THE BENEFICIARIES. HOLDING A READING OF THE WILL IS AN IDEAL OPPORTUNITY TO INFORM THE BENEFICIARIES OF PROCEDURES AND TO MANAGE THEIR EXPECTATIONS ABOUT HOW LONG THE ESTATE IS GOING TO TAKE.

Can an executor get away with ignoring the instructions in the will?

2,289 views

Here is another letter from a reader who, as you readers tend to do, hit the nail right on the head with a question that will interest many of you.

> *"What can be some ramifications of an executor who disregards instructions that have been written in the will? I assume they cannot just get away with doing whatever they want can they?"*

Executors get away with a heck of a lot, partly because they don't really know what they're doing and partly because the beneficiaries don't know either. This only gets worse when the executor either doesn't hire an experienced estate lawyer, or hires one and ignores his advice. A large number of executors are under the impression that the estate they are looking after has been given to them to do with as they see fit, including re-writing the parts of the will they don't especially like, and of course this leads to trouble.

I'm glad to see you asking questions about this because beneficiaries and families in general need to know more about the estate process. There is no government agency that oversees what executors are doing. It's up to the beneficiaries of an estate to keep the executor on the straight and narrow, but that's not easy to do when you don't really know what the rules are.

Yes, there can be ramifications for an executor who disregards the specifics of the will. The severity of the consequences will depend on the facts of the breach. For example, an executor might ignore the will's instructions to sell everything, and give the beneficiary an item without selling it first. That would be considered less serious than an executor who decides to keep all of the money in the estate for himself without giving anything to the beneficiaries.

If an executor has simply made a mistake and realizes it, the objective should be to fix it to the extent possible without any need to punish anyone. However, court involvement is usually required to bring about any consequences for an executor because few will admit they've done something wrong, and even fewer will volunteer to correct their mistakes. The severity of the penalty is decided by a judge. Some of the things that judges will do fairly often are:

- remove the executor from the job of being executor

- reduce the executor's fee or withhold it altogether

- force the executor to produce a decent accounting

- set deadlines for the executor to meet

- force an executor to pay back money out of his own pocket

If the executor refuses to do as the judge says, the judge might ramp up the consequences. This could mean holding the executor in contempt of court, which could mean a fine or jail time.

If an executor has stolen from an estate, he can be arrested just like anyone else. Depending on the facts, this could lead to fines or jail time or other punishments decided by the courts.

Lately I've posted a few times about new cases involving executors who have been held accountable for not following a will. The courts seem to be cracking down on them, and for the sake of the families and beneficiaries who are at the mercy of the executors, I'm happy to see it.

Will the judge remove the executor if I apply to the court?

4,831 views

The majority of the questions I received this week were from beneficiaries who are fed up with the executors in charge of estates in which they are involved. They said the executors are terrible and the beneficiaries want to go to court to have the executors removed. I can see their point. An awful lot of executors really are doing a terrible job, and some will no doubt be removed. I'd like to take a few minutes to take a closer look at this idea of a beneficiary applying to the court to remove an executor.

It's an uphill job. Nobody should think that getting an executor tossed out of an estate is quick or easy. First of all, there are two sides to every story (actually there are probably more like ten) and the court process for dealing with testimony can be lengthy. Assuming that the executor objects to being booted out of the job, there may be affidavits filed, counter-affidavits filed, examinations on affidavit (in-person cross examination of what you said in your affidavit) held, and undertakings given. This could take several months.

The real obstacle to removing an executor is the fact that he or she was chosen by the deceased. If a judge removes the executor, the judge is in effect re-writing part of the will. They don't take that lightly; in fact judges will make every effort to uphold the terms of the will as much as possible.

If you apply to the court to ask that the executor be removed, the judge has more options than simply saying yes or no to that request. In fact, the lawyer that helps you bring your application to court should know this, and suggest some of those less drastic options that might work for you as a back-up in case the judge does say no. The judge may try to get things back on track with the current executor.

For example, if the problem you're having with the executor is that she simply will not give any information and you believe that money has gone missing, the judge might order a passing of accounts. As another example, if your complaint is that the executor is simply dragging his heels and isn't doing anything at all, to the detriment of the estate, the judge might impose a deadline for taking certain steps. Depending on the issue, the judge could order the sale of a house, direct mediation between certain parties or set executor's compensation.

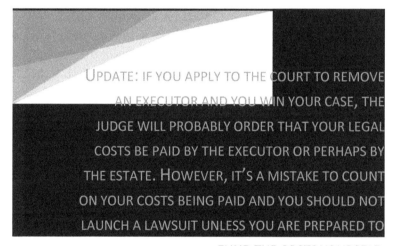

UPDATE: IF YOU APPLY TO THE COURT TO REMOVE AN EXECUTOR AND YOU WIN YOUR CASE, THE JUDGE WILL PROBABLY ORDER THAT YOUR LEGAL COSTS BE PAID BY THE EXECUTOR OR PERHAPS BY THE ESTATE. HOWEVER, IT'S A MISTAKE TO COUNT ON YOUR COSTS BEING PAID AND YOU SHOULD NOT LAUNCH A LAWSUIT UNLESS YOU ARE PREPARED TO FUND THE COSTS YOURSELF.

Keep in mind that if you're proposing that an executor be removed, you'd best have a replacement in mind. The best option would be an alternate named in the will, if there is one. The judge may not think that having an estate with no executor is good for the estate, and having nobody in charge definitely isn't going to resolve your concerns.

This is not to say that it's impossible to remove a rogue executor. It certainly does happen. It probably needs to happen more often than it does. Sometimes in the really egregious cases the executor ends up in jail either for theft from the estate or for contempt of the judge's orders. In other, less dramatic, cases the executor isn't jailed but is released from his or her duties, perhaps with costs assessed against him or her by the court.

I look at this as a positive thing. Yes, I'm a born optimist, I know that, but look at it this way. Maybe the only thing you can think of to fix a broken estate is to remove the executor. Seeing an experienced lawyer and getting in front of a judge brings you face to face two very knowledgeable people who can help you with that estate. They will suggest solutions that you might never have thought of.

Joint property

Frankly, I'm amazed at the number of questions I get about real estate, and the thousands upon thousands of readers who look at my posts about property. I often wonder whether the practice of real estate lawyers has been pared down to such efficiency that they don't have time to discuss the pros and cons of the forms of property ownership with their clients. People seem to be very poorly informed about the very homes they live in. Many certainly do not understand what will happen with the property once they pass away.

Not that all of the confusion can be blamed on the real estate lawyers, by any means. I've come to realize that our land titles system is much too easily accessed by people who think changing the title on their home is no more involved than changing their shoes. It seems not to register with them that once they put someone else on their title, they can't just kick them off again. I believe the vast majority of those questionable transactions were completed without the help of lawyers.

Some proportion of the questions I receive are not about what happens to property when someone passes away. They are about couples divorcing or common law couples splitting up, or other scenarios not involving estates. Generally, I feel that I cannot answer those questions because it wouldn't be fair to the people asking. I don't practice matrimonial law and I haven't worked in that area for many, many years. They would not be well-served by an answer from me. In those cases I have to ask them to find someone else – a lawyer with more skill and knowledge in that area of law - to answer the question.

One of the most common themes I deal with in terms of joint property is the issue of a parent adding a child to the title of the home or cabin. This is something I write about often and will continue to write about. Too many parents are unknowingly causing huge problems among their children by naively adding names to their property titles without understanding the possible consequences. The posts I write are, I'm glad to see, very well-read. It's such an important topic for so many families that I feel some urgency to get the message out there.

Joint tenants vs. tenants-in-common
200,618 views

When talking to clients about estate planning, I always ask them about the title to their homes, cottages and revenue properties. The majority of people will respond with the names of the people who are "on title". However, when I ask whether the people on title are on as joint tenants or as tenants-in-common, they usually don't know. I'm often then asked, "Does it make a difference?"

The short answer is yes, it makes a difference.

When a property is held in joint tenancy, the situation is what I refer to as "the last man standing". When one joint tenant dies, the entire property belongs to the remaining,

UPDATE: IT'S IMPORTANT TO UNDERSTAND THAT THE GENERAL RULES OF JOINT PROPERTY DON'T APPLY WHEN A PARENT ADDS A CHILD AS A JOINT OWNER ON A TITLE THAT THE PARENT ALREADY OWNS. MAKE SURE YOU READ ALL POSTS ABOUT JOINT PROPERTY AND THE POST BELOW ABOUT *MAKING AN INTER-GENERATIONAL JOINT TENANCY WORK* TO GET A FULL PICTURE OF WHAT SHOULD HAPPEN WHEN THE TITLE IS HELD JOINTLY BETWEEN PARENT AND CHILD, AND THE PARENT PASSES AWAY.

surviving joint tenant(s). Whoever is the last joint tenant to die owns the property. Only that last person can use his or her Will to give the property to someone else.

For example, let's say Robert, Dean and Chris are joint tenants of a house. Dean passes away. Even though Dean would like to leave his share to his wife, he can't because he's a joint tenant. Robert and Chris then own the property. Robert dies. Chris now owns the whole property. Because Chris is the only name on title now, he can leave the property to his wife and children. There is nothing for Dean or Robert's families.

Tenants-in-common is a different story. In this arrangement, each person owns a half, or third, or some other portion that belongs only to them. They can leave their share to someone in their Will or sell it (never mind the logistical problems of trying to sell one third of a house).

To adapt our example above, let's say Robert, Dean and Chris are tenants-in-common of the property and each owns and equal 1/3. When Dean passes away, he leaves his share to his wife, Deana. Now the owners are Robert, Deana and Chris. Then Robert passes away and leaves his shares to his wife, Roberta. Now the owners are Deana, Roberta and Chris. In this way, each of the individual owners retains control of his or her share.

Between a husband and wife, a title is almost always held as joint tenants. This is so that when the first spouse dies, the other one will automatically own the family home without having to go through probate. Note that this is not always done in second marriages, depending on the situation.

The subject of names on title comes up at estate planning time because the type of ownership might affect your estate plan.

What happens when a tenant-in-common dies?
9,256 views

In this blog, I've mentioned a few times (and will mention many more times, I'm sure) what happens when a joint owner of property dies. However, I was recently asked what happens when a tenant-in-common dies.

A major difference between joint owners and tenants-in-common is that joint owners automatically have a right of survivorship to the entire property. Even though there are two or more joint owners, they are all considered owners of the entire property, as opposed to a half or a third. There are no halves or thirds with joint owners.

With tenants-in-common there ARE halves and thirds (and other portions). Each person owns only a portion of the property, according to the Transfer of Land document that was filed with the Land Titles Office when they acquired the property. There is no right of survivorship with tenants-in-common because each owner owns his or her section only.

It's possible for two people to be joint tenants of one portion of a tenancy-in-common.

When a tenant-in-common dies, his or her portion of the land is dealt with like any other asset that is in that person's name alone. Hopefully the person has a Will which sets out who will get his or her property. If not, there will be an administrator appointed by the court. Whoever is the beneficiary of the estate will become the new owner of the deceased's portion of the property. The portions of the property owned by the other tenants-in-common are not directly affected.

When deciding whether you want to own property as joint owners or tenants-in-common, or whether you want to own real estate together with other people at all, you really do have to think through the likely scenarios you might encounter. For example, if you own 1/3 of a house as a tenant-in-common and you want to sell your share, how do you get out of the arrangement? How do you sell 1/3 of a house? Are the other tenants-in-common in a position to buy you out?

If a new owner does join the tenancy-in-common because he or she has inherited someone's portion, how will the other owners interact with that person? Will they be able to agree on issues such as whether it should be sold, who should live in the house, etc.?

There are pluses and minuses for different possible arrangements, and each comes with its own set of owner's rights. When I ask clients about their ownership arrangements, the vast majority say that they don't know whether they are joint owners or tenants-in-common. You should make sure that you thoroughly understand your own situation.

How do I sell my half of a jointly owned house?
49,368 views

The fact that I'm asked this question so frequently hammers home a couple of points for me. One is that people don't understand the nature of joint ownership. The second is that parents should stop leaving their house to all of their children jointly.

When two (or more) people own a property as joint tenants, there is a right of survivorship. This means that each of them owns the entire property, just as both would own every dollar in a joint bank account. There is no "half" in a jointly owned property. Each owns 100%. Therefore, there is no "half" to sell.

This seems to be a really tough concept for people. I'm constantly asked about this issue on my blog and at pretty much every seminar I present. One person argued with me for about ten minutes about the fact that if two people owned a house it HAD to be half and half. He had no legal reason to believe this, but that didn't stop him from being absolutely sure that he'd know this better than I would.

The whole idea behind a joint ownership is to leave the entire property to the other person when one dies. For example, if a husband and wife own their home jointly and one of them dies, the other still has the house. It's a "last man standing" concept. It doesn't really work for a number of siblings owning a house.

If two or more people want to own "halves" or "parts" of a house, they should hold that property as tenants in common. In that arrangement, each has a piece of the house that he or she can sell or leave to someone in their Will.

194

This brings me to the second point.

About 90% of the questions I get about how to get out of a joint tenancy come from people who own something with their siblings and the arrangement isn't working. It's almost always because a parent left the house to ALL of the children equally. Parents need to be realistic about the million or so ways this arrangement can go wrong. More than one child wants to live there, and nobody can agree. One moves in but won't move out and won't pay rent or expenses. The roof needs repairs but each wants the others to pay for it. One rents it out without the permission of the others. One causes damage and won't pay for repairs. Two want to sell but the third won't sign. And on and on and on.

Why wouldn't the parents choose one child to take the house as part of his share? Or direct that the house be sold and the proceeds split? This is truly something done without thought that leads to so many fights and headaches, I can't believe anyone does this anymore. Parents - please stop doing this to your kids!

How to make an intergenerational joint tenancy work
2,642 views

It's great that people are reading my warnings about using joint tenancy as an estate-planning tool without legal advice. This question from a reader gives me a reason to go a little deeper into the issue of intergenerational joint tenancy.

> *"I live with my mom in her principal residence. It is paid for and she has no debt. She intends to pass on the house to me after her passing, and her remaining assets divided up equally amongst the other siblings. Having read some of your other articles regarding inter-generational joint tenancy not working as true joint tenancy, what is the best and most definitive way for her to pass on her house to me without having to incur probate cost and deal with unwanted conflicts from other siblings?"*

A parent who wants to leave his or her home to one of the children has a couple of options. There is never one right answer or arrangement that suits everyone.

You are right that if your Mom doesn't add you as a joint tenant on the property, and the property is in her name alone when she passes away, it will be necessary to probate her will in order to transfer the house. Adding you as a joint tenant might or might not keep the house out of probate - more on that in a moment - but even if it did keep the house out, the chances are good that your Mom's will would have to be probated anyway if there are other assets.

If your Mom wants to add you as a joint tenant on her house so that you inherit the house on her death, it can be

196

done. Yes, you are right that intergenerational joint tenancies don't automatically operate as true joint tenancies any more, but there is more to that general rule. If there is evidence provided by the parent at the time the property was made joint, this may well serve to create a joint tenancy that will properly hold up. This is why I always tell people not to put the house in joint names without legal advice, because the lawyer will help the parent document those intentions in the right way.

So, your Mom can add you as a joint tenant on the house and document her intentions. To make that even stronger, your Mom can make a new will close to the time she changes the title on the house and confirm her intentions in the will. As mentioned, this might not avoid probate for the other assets of the estate but it would keep the house out of probate. That would keep probate fees lower.

Conflict from other siblings is an issue that causes untold damage and I think you and your Mom are smart to think about the optics of leaving the house to you. The way I read your question, I concluded that you get the house and your siblings divide the rest, without you getting a share of "the rest". I don't know what the monetary value is, but given your concern over conflict, I assume they'll be getting less than you will in terms of value. Is there a reason why your Mom wants to give you more? Have you been the one who has always helped her, or do you already live in the house? Has your Mom already given financial help to the others? Even a brief statement in the will that explains her actions can have a calming effect. I am talking about a statement that starts off with "I love all of my children equally but I am leaving a bit larger share to Child X because..." followed by one or two lines explaining her reason.

Also, your Mom needs to clarify whether getting the house means also getting the contents of the house along with the title. Personal items are the cause of more fights than money is, so she needs to be VERY clear on whether your siblings can take anything out of the house.

This is not a will that your Mom should be making on her own. She should talk to a lawyer who specializes in wills and estate planning to discuss the wording of the will and the implications of an intergenerational joint tenancy.

Can't sell the deceased's house because the other joint owner is also deceased - now what?

2,380 views

This reader wrote to me after what appears to be years of frustration with trying to deal with two entwined estates. At the root of the issue is the fact that a joint owner of a house did not take steps to update the title after the other joint owner died. Toss in a lost will and you have an interesting situation. Neither a lost will nor a failure to deal with a land title is at all uncommon, so I thought I'd share this reader's dilemma here.

Here is the question (or should I call it a cry of desperation?):

> *"I hope beyond hope you can help me. Grandfather died in 1988. Grandmother was co-owner of the house. Aunt was named executrix of Grandfather's will. Aunt lost the original will. We have copies. The will wasn't probated. Grandmother died in 2001. Her estate was probated and dealt with, except for house (paid off) which we cannot sell due to joint ownership. Not one lawyer will touch this. Not sure where to start. HELP!"*

This isn't really that complicated. If no lawyer will touch it, it's because you're asking the wrong lawyers. Find someone who specializes in wills and estates by calling the Canadian Bar Association (not the Law Society) in your province. You can also google wills and estates lawyers, then read the profiles of lawyers in your area to determine whether they have the necessary experience.

In order to proceed with the sale of the house, first your grandfather's name must come off the title. To do that, your aunt needs to probate your grandfather's will so that his executor will have the legal ability to sign documents on his behalf. If the original has been lost, she needs to try to probate a copy of it. That isn't done often, but can be done in certain circumstances with the permission of the court. It's more complicated than probating an original, but not impossible.

If your aunt is reluctant to act, you might remind her that she may be personally responsible (i.e. not covered by the estate but out of her own pocket) for any loss that occurs to the house, loss of rent since 2001, any capital gains tax that accrues while the house is waiting to be sold, and any court costs/lawyer's fees if you have to force her to take steps. Perhaps she would find that information to be motivational.

It wouldn't have been necessary for your grandfather's will to be probated if your grandmother had taken your grandfather's name off the title herself after he died. She, like any surviving joint tenant, could have simply gone to the land titles office with a death certificate and had the title changed over to her name alone. But since she didn't, and may have had no idea that she could even do that, now probate is needed so that someone has legal authority to deal with the title.

Once your aunt obtains probate, she will have the legal authority to take your grandfather's name off the title. After that, the executor of your grandmother's estate can arrange to sell the property. The proceeds will go into the grandmother's estate, not the grandfather's estate.

This situation isn't really all that unusual, in the sense that surviving joint tenants often don't realize that they have to do anything with the title to their home. They understand that when one joint tenant dies, the other automatically owns the house. The word "automatically" is misleading, as it implies that no action needs to be taken. More accurately, the surviving joint tenant has the right of ownership, but must make sure that the title record is brought up to date at the land titles office.

In your case, the loss of the original will does complicate things somewhat, but it's not impossible to deal with. The key for you is going to be finding someone with the required depth of knowledge in this area of law.

Power of attorney and elder law

Posts about powers of attorney have not been as popular as posts about executorship. I suppose that's to be expected on a blog with "estate" in its name. However, more and more people are beginning to look for information about powers of attorney simply because more and more of them are being faced with the need for them as their parents get older.

Because of the aging of the Baby Boomers, we as a society are going to see a huge upsurge in the use of powers of attorney. I certainly hope that this upsurge will be accompanied by good legal advice and competent documents. I'll be doing my bit to answer questions for those who don't know where else to turn.

Posts that are always popular are news stories about family members who are caught and punished for abuse of their elder family members, whether that abuse is physical or financial. I think these stories hit awfully close to home, since we all have parents. As our parents age, many are in the hands of paid caregivers, which causes the children guilt and worry. We somehow feel that parents should be safer and more cherished when cared for by their own relatives, and seeing stories where the opposite is true tends to shock and horrify us.

I sometimes put up links to that kind of news story to remind readers to keep an eye on any seniors they know who are being cared for but may not have friends or confidantes close by.

Can a power of attorney change a beneficiary designation?

5,153 views

I was asked this question yesterday when speaking to a group of Sunlife financial advisors, and in fact I'm asked it pretty often. The question is whether an attorney acting under an Enduring Power of Attorney can change an existing beneficiary designation on behalf of the person he or she represents. For example, if Haley is acting as attorney for her Dad, and Dad has a RRIF that designates his two children as the beneficiaries, can Haley change that?

UPDATE: THIS IS THE KIND OF PRACTICAL INFORMATION PEOPLE USING POWERS OF ATTORNEY SEEM TO BE SEEKING. I ALWAYS ENCOURAGE THIS KIND OF "HOW-TO" QUESTION.

Beneficiary designations are found on RRIFs, RRSPs, LIRAs, segregated funds, pensions, insurance policies and other instruments.

The answer is "no", the attorney cannot legally change an existing beneficiary designation. It doesn't matter if the attorney agrees with the designation or not; it's not the attorney's money or the attorney's decision.

It's possible that an investment that has a designated beneficiary might mature, and the attorney has to take steps

203

to re-invest it on behalf of the person he or she represents. In this case, the attorney's job is to continue the designation that had been made before. Deciding not to continue the designation is the same as deliberately changing it.

What may a person acting under a Power of Attorney charge?

6,031 views

If you are acting under an Enduring Power of Attorney, you may be handling assets of all descriptions, and taking on the responsibility for important financial matters. You may be taking time away from work or your family. Do you know whether you are being paid for this work and responsibility? If so, do you know how much you should be charging?

To find out where you stand, look first to the Enduring Power of Attorney document itself. Does it say anything about compensation? The rules and guidelines for payment of an individual acting under a Power of Attorney vary across Canada. In some provinces, the law allows compensation for all Attorneys (note that in Canada, the word "attorney" does not mean a lawyer; it means a person acting under a Power of Attorney). In other provinces (e.g. B.C.) the law says that the Attorney may only be paid if the document itself says so.

I have always encouraged my clients to think about whether they want their Attorney to be paid, and if so, how much. The documents I've prepared have always addressed this. This is partly because I want to avoid disputes among family members later on. Families tend to have the "if Dad wanted you to be paid, he'd have said so" folks in one camp, and the "he didn't say so because it was assumed that I'd be paid" folks in another.

I still think talking about compensation in the Power of Attorney itself is the best idea. It shows that the person who signed the document thought about the question and decided what is fair. I like the idea that the clients are fully informed of how the document may be used, and the implications of that.

Determining how much an Attorney may be paid is not as easy as figuring out what an executor is going to be paid. An executor is paid only once, at the end of his or her executorship, on a percentage of probatable assets in existence on the date of death. That formula won't really work for Attorneys.

Part of the problem is that we can't know ahead of time whether the incapacity that brings the Power of Attorney into play is a short-term issue or a long-term problem. Sometimes children act as the Attorney for their parent for years. When would the payment be calculated? Once a year? Once a month?

The calculation itself may present challenges, as the assets being managed will likely change over time.

In Ontario, there is a rate prescribed by law that is a combination of a percentage of capital and revenue receipts, a percentage of disbursements, and an annual care and management fee. If nothing is said in the Power of Attorney document, this rate applies. The person making the Power of Attorney may change it if he or she wishes. Other provinces (e.g. Alberta) have only a guideline that says that an Attorney may take "fair and reasonable" compensation.

In many Enduring Powers of Attorney, a small monthly amount (say $100 to $200) has been named as the wages the Attorney can expect to receive. It is more of an honorarium than a wage, which in my opinion makes sense, as the Attorney is not likely to work full-time at being an Attorney. The amount is paid monthly to accommodate the fact that sometimes the Attorney's job lasts for a few months and in other case it will be years, so someone who works longer will be paid more. If there is more than one Attorney acting, they will have to split the amount.

Some Attorneys will choose not to accept payment, even if it is offered, and this is something that you will have to decide for yourself based on your unique situation. A family member might refuse payment if he or she feels an obligation to help parents or other relatives. The fact that the compensation must be included in a personal tax return as earned income might also affect the decision.

In some provinces (e.g. Ontario, Manitoba), the law says that an Attorney who is paid for being an attorney is held to a higher standard of accountability for his or her actions. The paid Attorney must show the same care and skill of a person who is in the business of managing the property of others. That might just be an impossible standard for someone who is acting as Attorney because he or she is the only available relative, but who has absolutely no experience or skill in money management.

Can Power of Attorney add himself to a bank account?

4,681 views

The scope of the powers of an attorney under an Enduring Power of Attorney, Continuing Power of Attorney, Durable Power of Attorney, or Power of Attorney for Property continues to be a mystery for many. This is why I'm always glad to receive questions about it.

Recently I was asked whether a person acting under a Power of Attorney can add himself to a bank account, presumably a bank account of the person he represents. The answer is both "yes" and "no", depending on what you mean by "add himself".

The idea of a Power of Attorney is to give someone else access to your money on your behalf. It's not in any way intended to give someone else ownership of your money or allow them to use it for themselves. So if "adding himself" to an account means that he becomes able to deposit your money, pay your bills, direct your investments, etc., then yes, he can add himself. This is what he is supposed to do for you.

As I said, Power of Attorney does not convey any ownership. Therefore if "adding himself" means putting his name on the account as a joint owner, then no he cannot add himself. Putting his name on as a joint owner means he has taken ownership of the money, as either owner of a joint account has the legal right to all of the money in the account.

In fact, it's possible that the Power of Attorney was made specifically to avoid anyone putting the assets into joint names.

208

Using a Power of Attorney to gain ownership of some or all of someone else's money is fraud or theft, depending on the circumstances. There is a special crime in Canada's Criminal Code called Theft by Person With Power of Attorney. The only reason more people don't blow the whistle on the activity of fraudulent use of Power of Attorney is that, as I said earlier, most people don't really understand the nuances of how it works.

UPDATE: THIS QUESTION ILLUSTRATES JUST HOW UNFAMILIAR MOST PEOPLE ARE WITH POWER OF ATTORNEY DOCUMENTS. IT'S WORTH YOUR WHILE TO SPEND AN HOUR WITH A LAWYER TO FIND OUT WHAT YOU CAN AND CANNOT DO WITH THE DOCUMENT.

Mom's in a nursing home; can we sell her house and divide the money?

5,351 views

Do you believe that other people should be allowed to take your money away from you - and I'm talking hundreds of thousands of dollars - because you are old and they think you don't need it? Of course not! So why do so many people think they can help themselves to their parents' estates without permission before the parents even pass away?

Here is a note I recently received from a reader:

> *"My mother has just been panelled to a Nursing Home. We are 5 children and one is her POA, and executor. Her will says that the house is to be sold and divided between the 5 children. Is it not best to sell the house right away and divide the money between the children, rather than keep it in a seperate account till she passes?"*

Would it be best to sell the house and divide the money right away? Best for whom? And why are you following the will of someone who isn't dead?

This is a subject that I've been asked about many times over the years, and I have to confess that it irritates me no end. Your mother's will says that the five of you are to inherit the proceeds of the sale of the house <u>after she passes away</u>. That's what wills do; they talk about what happens to an estate after a person dies. She hasn't passed away. Therefore, no, you can't have the money.

The executor has <u>zero</u> power to do anything at all while your mother is alive. The will has no effect while your mother is alive. So nobody gets to act as her executor yet. Forget the executor and the will while your mother is still alive. I hope I've made this point clearly enough, not just for you but for all of the other readers who ask me this question repeatedly.

Now let's look at the attorney acting under the Power of Attorney (POA). Has the POA been brought into effect? Don't assume that because your mother is going to a nursing home that the POA is automatically in effect. Going into a home likely has no effect on it at all. The person named in the document should read it carefully to see what has to happen to spring it into effect. In many provinces that means having a doctor sign a declaration of incapacity.

Once the attorney under the POA has properly sprung the document into effect, the attorney has to do what is in the best interest of your mother. Maybe this means selling the house. If your mother is never going to be able to live there again, then perhaps that's the best thing to do financially. However - and this point is NOT to be overlooked - the sale proceeds of the house must be invested for your mother. The attorney under the POA does not have the legal right to distribute the funds to you five. He or she risks financial penalties, removal from the job of POA and perhaps even jail time for that, depending on the circumstances.

Rarely do posts move me to use quite as much underlining as I've used in this one, but this topic is so important. Over and over again, I see children with an over-inflated sense of entitlement taking money that doesn't belong to them on the philosophy that "one day it will be theirs". That day hasn't arrived yet.

Mom's showing signs of dementia, should I get power of attorney for her? 2,629 views

All of us whose parents have reached a certain age notice if our parents begin to show the early signs of memory loss or disorientation. It may be distressing or alarming, but no matter how we feel about it, we ask ourselves what we are supposed to do when this happens. A reader recently asked me the following question:

> *"My mother has me as an executor in her will. She is showing signs of senility. Should I consider getting a power of attorney for my mom now before things get worse? My dad is even older, but not showing signs of senility."*

The parents in this family are lucky that they have a child who is alert to changes and willing to offer the help necessary. The fact that this child is the executor is not relevant to the question, except that the executor appointment shows that the parents trust the child to deal with legal matters.

Yes, I believe that these parents should have powers of attorney documents put into place, assuming they are still able to understand and sign them. The type of document needed is often called "enduring" or "continuing", or "power of attorney for property". This type of power of attorney, unlike the regular business power of attorney, is designed to last or continue even though its maker might lose mental capacity after the document is made.

The reader mentions that the father seems not to have any signs of incapacity. I would recommend that both parents prepare documents now and not wait until the father also begins to lose his capacity. I also recommend that the parents consider signing health care directives to put someone in charge of medical and personal decisions should that become necessary.

A question that will have to be addressed is whether the power of attorney document is to come into effect immediately or to come into effect at a future date. The future date is the date that the parent loses mental capacity. Often when a parent is already demonstrating signs of memory loss, the best option is to have the document come into effect right away. In this reader's situation, perhaps the mother's power of attorney should come into effect immediately but the father's document should come into effect in the future if he should need it. This is something that can be decided between the parents and their lawyer at the time the documents are prepared.

A significant issue addressed in this reader's question is that of acting now before things get worse. Typically, seniors with dementia or Alzheimer's disease do deteriorate (remember I'm a lawyer, not a doctor, and I'm speaking only from my personal observations). Therefore, if you wait too long to act, the opportunity to have legal documents prepared may well be lost. A person must have mental capacity to sign legal documents. Capacity doesn't have to be perfect, and most seniors who are in the early stages of deterioration are still capable of signing documents.

If a senior sees a lawyer to have wills or powers of attorney prepared, the lawyer will assess the senior for capacity. An experienced lawyer will know that a person who is beginning to demonstrate incapacity will have good days and bad days, and will do everything she can to maximize the senior's likelihood of having a good day. For example, the lawyer might meet the senior at the senior's home rather than asking the senior to come downtown, which could be disorienting.

It's clear that the child in this question understands the importance of a power of attorney. It also sounds like he or she is willing to act as the attorney in that document. However, it's essential to remember that whether the document is prepared and the choice of attorney are decisions that belong to the parent. The child can raise the subject and provide practical help like a ride to the lawyer's office, but ultimately it's up to the parents to sign or not sign documents.

UPDATE: DON'T EVER ASK AN ELDERLY PERSON TO SIGN A DOCUMENT THAT YOU KNOW THEY DON'T REALLY UNDERSTAND. NOT ONLY WILL THE DOCUMENT BE INVALID, BUT YOU COULD ALSO END UP IN LEGAL TROUBLE IF YOU PERSONALLY GAIN IN ANY WAY FROM THE DOCUMENT.

The parents might choose someone else to act under the power of attorney, so the reader should be prepared for that.

Despite the fact that time becomes the enemy once incapacity begins to emerge, try not to rush elderly parents into specific decisions. Rushing them often results in nothing but upsetting or frightening them, so be patient.

If you have Power of Attorney you don't need a joint account

3,377 views

Powers of Attorney continue to be poorly understood by the people who are forced to rely on them. I was reminded of this over the weekend when I spent some time talking with someone who couldn't understand why his parents' bank wouldn't let him use his parents' Power of Attorney to put his name on his parents' accounts as a joint owner.

My first thought when hearing about this scenario was that if you have a Power of Attorney you already have full access to the account. You can already do everything you need to do, such as pay bills, deposit money, roll over investments and obtain paperwork. So why would you need to be added as a joint account holder?

The big difference between having Power of Attorney access to the account and joint owner access to the account is ownership. When using a Power of Attorney you are supposed to be using the account to carry out financial transactions to benefit your parents, and you don't own the asset. When you add your name as a joint account holder, you are basically giving the money to yourself as all joint owners own the funds. That's hardly in your parents' best interest, is it?

A Power of Attorney doesn't give you the right to take assets for yourself. In fact that's the very opposite of what a Power of Attorney does.

Of course the bank isn't going to allow you to use a Power of Attorney to give your parents' money to yourself. Given the epidemic of elder financial abuse, I applaud the bank for being vigilant and knowing the limits of a Power of

215

Attorney document. I'm sure that in this case there was no fraudulent intent by the child holding the Power of Attorney, but the bank doesn't know that, and was right to refuse the request.

At this point in the conversation, the child holding the Power of Attorney protests that he or she only wants to be added to the account to help the parents with financial transactions. But as I said at the beginning, the Power of Attorney does that for you.

I have heard of a growing movement among lawyers to suggest to their clients that they include a certain clause in their Powers of Attorney. The clause would say that the person they are naming under the Power of Attorney would not be able to use the document until they had spent an hour with a lawyer learning about what they could and could not do. I'm completely in favour of that.

Other books by Lynne Butler

Protect Your Elderly Parents: Become Your
Parent's Guardian or Trustee
*Available at Chapters, Amazon, and from Self-
Counsel Press*

Succession Planning Kit for Canadian Business
*Available at Chapters, Amazon, and from Self-
Counsel Press*

Estate Planning Through Family Meetings
*Available at Chapters, Amazon, and from Self-
Counsel Press*

Alberta Probate Kit
*Available at Chapters, Amazon, and from Self-
Counsel Press*

The Beneficiary's Answer Book
Available from lulu.com

How Executors Avoid Personal Liability
*Available at Chapters, Amazon, and from Self-
Counsel Press*

For My Family, With Love
Available from lulu.com

To read more of Lynne Butler's blog posts, go to
www.estatelawcanada.blogspot.ca

Feel free to leave feedback about this book, or about any topic posted.

Your comments and questions are welcome.

See you there!

☐

To find out how you can hire Lynne Butler
to assist you
with a legal matter respecting a will or
estate,
visit her webpage at
www.butlerwillsandestates.com

CPSIA information can be obtained
at www.ICGtesting.com
Printed in the USA
LVHW111805120121
676308LV00004B/542

9 781329 650756